Lillian's *Survival and Conscience: From the Shadows of Nazi Germany to the Jewish Boat to Gaza* is a powerful narrative that is written with boundless humanity and dignity. Her life's journey is that of discovery, in which morality and human rights played a central role in her thinking, but more importantly in her actions. *Survival and Conscience* is a testament to the triumph of the human spirit over the confines of the narrow definitions of group identity and politics, where collective traumas are manipulated to exploit and subjugate others. Lillian's book is penned with the poise of an intellectual, but with the heart of a poet—unpretentious, refined, and profound. I strongly recommend this book.

DR. RAMZY BAROUD,
Editor of *Palestine Chronicle* and
author, *My Father Was A Freedom Fighter*

I truly admire Lillian Rosengarten for her activism, steadfastness and especially for writing this very important and touching book. I got to know Lillian as an extraordinary and very educated person, deeply influenced by her own and her family's awful experiences in Nazi Germany. Facing the challenges of fleeing Nazi Germany as a young girl made her understand that all forms of extreme nationalism and racism are dangerous and must be combated. Because this attitude is reflected in every line of her book, it is a must-read for everyone concerned with the Middle East and the Israeli-Palestinian conflict!

ANNETTE GROTH,
Left Party Member of the Bundestag from Baden-Württemberg

A committed human rights activist, poet, writer, psychoanalyst, world traveler, Jew, and pacifist, Lillian writes with passion and detailed honesty. Her memoir is a cry from the heart, a call for the centrality of human rights for all. Her experience with near annihilation as a child, her personal struggles with grief and guilt, and her life long search for justice and spiritual peace is both moving and inspiring. Her willingness to bear witness to the "squalid hell" in Gaza and to get on that boat is a rousing shout to action. Lillian is unafraid to state that for her, the Palestinians are the final victims of the Nazi Holocaust; holding Israel accountable is both an act of desperation and love.

ALICE ROTHCHILD
Author, *On the Brink: Israel and Palestine on the Eve of the 2014 Gaza Invasion*

Lillian Rosengarten has done something incredible in *Survival and Conscience.* By ruthlessly examining her family's "exodus from Germany" during the Holocaust, she comes to understand the ways that Nazi persecution helped produce mental illness inside her family. But then she breaks down the personal wall of that experience, and by venturing on the Jewish Boat to Gaza, explains its connection to Israel's persecution of the Palestinians. She has produced a brave and wrenching account that is also deeply necessary, as Americans seek to understand how we joined our country's interests with Israel's.

PHILIP WEISS
Founder and managing editor, *Mondoweiss*

Survival and Conscience

Just World Books
Timely Books for Changing Times

Just World Books exists to expand the discourse in the United States and worldwide on issues of vital international concern. We are committed to building a more just, equitable, and peaceable world. We uphold the equality of all human persons. We aim for our books to contribute to increasing understanding across national, religious, ethnic, and racial lines; to share more broadly the reflections, analyses, and policy prescriptions of pathbreaking activists for peace; and to help to prevent war.

To learn about our existing and upcoming titles, to find our terms for bookstores or other bulk purchasers, or to buy our books, visit our website:

www.JustWorldBooks.com

Also, follow us on Facebook, Twitter, and Instagram!

Our recent titles include:

- *The People Make the Peace*, edited by Karín Aguilar-San Juan and Frank Joyce
- *Gaza Unsilenced*, edited by Refaat Alareer and Laila El-Haddad
- *Baddawi*, by Leila Abdelrazaq
- *Chaos and Counterrevolution: After the Arab Spring*, by Richard Falk
- *Palestine: The Legitimacy of Hope*, by Richard Falk
- *Chief Complaint: A Country Doctor's Tales of Life in Galilee*, by Hatim Kanaaneh
- *In Our Power: U.S. Students Organize for Justice in Palestine*, by Nora Barrows-Friedman
- *Gaza Writes Back: Short Stories from Young Writers in Gaza, Palestine*, edited by Refaat Alareer
- *The Gaza Kitchen: A Palestinian Culinary Journey*, by Laila El-Haddad and Maggie Schmitt
- *On the Brink: Israel and Palestine on the Eve of the 2014 Gaza Invasion*, by Alice Rothchild
- *The General's Son: Journey of an Israeli in Palestine*, by Miko Peled

Survival and *Conscience*

From the Shadows of Nazi Germany to the Jewish Boat to Gaza

Lillian Rosengarten

Just World Books
Charlottesville, Virginia

Timely Books for Changing Times

Just World Books is an imprint of Just World Publishing, LLC.

Front cover image courtesy of Lillian Rosengarten
Cover design and typesetting by Diana Ghazzawi for Just World Publishing, LLC.
Photos in Chapter 8 by Vish Vishvanath.

Publisher's Cataloging in Publication

(Provided by Quality Books, Inc.)

Rosengarten, Lillian, author.
    Survival and conscience : from the shadows of Nazi
Germany to the Jewish boat to Gaza / Lillian
Rosengarten.
    pages cm
    LCCN 2015947660
    ISBN 978-1-935982-60-9
    ISBN 978-1-935982-63-0

    1. Rosengarten, Lillian. 2. Holocaust survivors--
United States--Biography. 3. Human rights workers--
United States--Biography. 4. Human rights advocacy.
5. Arab-Israel conflict--1993- 6. Autobiographies.
I. Title.

DS134.42.R668A3 2015   940.53'18092

QBI15-600170

For Lydia, Daniel, Melina, Emilia, and the memory of Philip
and to the courageous activists on
the Jewish Boat to Gaza, *Irene*, September 2010,
Edith, Eli, Itamar, Glyn, Rami, Reuven, Vish, Yonatan
Love,
Lillian

Wild Mother's Lament for Dead Children

Lillian Rosengarten

What is this strange world where children die?
Question the killers, suffering everywhere.
Callous indifference deadened in pursuit of blood.
Little screams on still faces. I cannot hear you! Speak.
Thousands of children, stench of burnt flesh, life without value.
Missiles slam smoldering in the moonlight.
I am your murderer nailed in a coffin of hate.
I am your mother stooped in grief. I am your father's vacant eyes.
I am the children.
Remember the spring of our years before a troubled twilight
Crushed you in a sea of tears?
Once I held you in my arms to suckle you with tenderness.
I had three children; one is dead.
I had eight children, four are dead or two or eight or all of them.
There is a fire, burns across the earth
Mixed with the blood of death.
They are all our children and we their parents.
War! Trampler of the soul. Death to the poets and lullabies.
How do they do it, arrogance of the armies?
Philip, do you even know you left last century behind,
Twin towers melted in flames turned to dust.
Wild with grief, we cry for lost children.
They were to make a better world.
Nightgown wrapped to suffocate.
I tear it from my body soaked in sweat.

As if to free myself from death or something else.
I dreamed a fire scorched the earth. Wild woman trapped.
Hold me, I am cold.
Ism'al our child, how cruelly you were taken
I am your spirit mother guarding a legacy.
Is the world listening?

Bisan, Mayar, Aya, Philip, Nur Abuelaish, you are our dead children.
Now we shall be your storytellers, your painter of dreams.
We will paint your canvas
Filled with details and memories.
We must be the keepers of the earth.

Contents

Foreword

"It is a complicated question," writes Lillian Rosengarten in the opening of this heartfelt, courageous memoir, "how a hunted people have become hunters, how victims became victimizers." It is a bold, challenging question, and it is the right question, the one that must be asked as we confront the most longstanding and systematic abuse of human rights in the world today. The personal and the political converge, Lillian points out early in this exploration of a life that spans Germany in the 1930s, New York in the last half of the twentieth century, and Gaza in the early twenty-first. In her courageous and intelligent book, Lillian invites us to accompany her in her quest for identity, personal wholeness, and the formation of a mission.

Although I was born a decade after Lillian, in postwar America rather than in Nazi Germany, it has not been difficult for me to identify with her personal, psychological, and political journey. "I have struggled," Lillian writes, "to organize the sequence of my personal and political life, both inextricably intertwined. To do so has required I scrutinize my life unflinchingly in order to examine deeply personal traumas with openness and honesty." Lillian grew up in a home that was profoundly colored by the pain, loss, and horror of the Nazi genocide. My own parents had not escaped personally from Hitler's clutches, but the DNA of Jewish suffering, marginalization, and fear operated strongly in my upbringing and in the forming of my consciousness. I was taught that in a world implacably and eternally bent on the destruction of the Jewish people, I had two enemies in particular: the Germans because of what they had done to us, and the "Arabs," as we called them, because of what they would do to us if we didn't have Israel. This sensibility of vulnerability, and the identity that is built upon it, is not limited to the past—it is always present. Effectively, we have remained trapped in our history of suffering; it colors our view of the present and dominates our vision of the future. Our stubborn commitment to the idea of an ethnic nationalist fortress state in the heart of the Middle East is evidence of how tragically trapped we are in this identity of victimhood.

"We know Jews have suffered and have been victims," Lillian writes. "Is it that mentality behind the walls Israel has built? Are they still 'victims' of paranoia and fear?"

The answer to this question is an unqualified "yes." Nine summers ago, I stood for the first time before the obscene wall of concrete that Israel has built through the heart of Palestine and recognized it as the wall that had been placed in my own heart growing up. I had met the Palestinians and realized that they did not hate me. I knew that eventually and inevitably they would get their freedom. It was, I understood with profound sadness, the Jewish citizens of Israel, and in a real sense the entire Jewish people, who were the real prisoners of that wall. That same summer, visiting Yad Vashem, Israel's memorial to the Jewish victims of Nazism, I came to the same realization expressed by Lillian in this book, making the same "obscene" analogy, the one we are never supposed to make. Here is Lillian, speaking with all the authority and all the credentials one needs to arrive at this conclusion:

> Nationalism revisited is now twisted into a parody of the Nazi credo, "Deutschland über alles," extolling Germany over all others, with only pure Germans as inhabitants. "Get rid of the undesirables who are beneath contempt!" I must not make such a comparison, you say. Yet I must, for I fear a Jewish State that belongs only to Jews is a dangerous road.... The cycle of paranoia and abuse is playing out its destructive course: this is how I understand Palestinians as the last victims of the Holocaust.

Reading this book was like looking into a mirror. Like Lillian, I have been haunted by the question of how we as a people can recover from our collective and historical trauma—from loss, dispossession, dehumanization. One option, well documented by psychologists who study and treat trauma, is to pass that same treatment on. As Jewish liberation theologian Marc Ellis has observed, our eternal victimhood has made us "innocent" of any wrongdoing. When Lillian stepped onto that boat bound for Gaza, she was acknowledging, as someday the Jewish people and indeed the rest of humanity will do, that Israel is not a victim but a victimizer, a state that must be held accountable for its criminal actions. With the question of Israel/ Palestine only increasing in urgency, what is the proper relationship of the rest of humankind to the Jewish people and to our national homeland project? Where does this leave those Jews who today find themselves torn between their commitment to religious and racial equality and their loyalty and attachment to the State of Israel? Where does this leave Christians, committed to social justice and to opposing oppression and racism wherever they are found, but still desiring to maintain hard-won ties of trust and reconciliation with the Jewish people? What must we do as a Jewish community as we struggle with the agony of our situation in historic Palestine? What is the future we want to create for ourselves?

Lillian Rosengarten's book points clearly to the course we must follow: calling Israel to account through nonviolent direct action, opening the way for Israel to join the community of nations in adherence to international law and fundamental principles of human rights. Like the global movement that liberated South Africans, white and black alike, from the evil of apartheid, pursuing the same goal for Israel is an act of love. Lillian's unwavering commitment to decency and compassion shine a light and provide the propulsion for action. More boats will sail for Gaza. The movement for boycott, divestment, and sanctions will continue to gain momentum.

Lillian's story transcends that of one family, one woman, one human rights struggle. What is the future we want to create for ourselves? It is Lillian Rosengarten, inviting us to step boldly with her into the future. It is a future fraught with uncertainty, singed with anger, touched with profound sadness, and holding a fierce hope.

Mark Braverman
Executive Director, Kairos USA

Prologue

A question runs through this book and asks how two major events of my life, two seemingly diametrically opposed experiences, have influenced one another to shape my opposition to Zionism. This is the story I wish to tell.

In 1936, my parents, Fritz and Lilli Lebrecht, found a way to leave their beloved Germany to flee the Nazis. Brownshirts had already started to terrorize the lives of Jews, including my parents. It was difficult for my father, who had left months earlier for New York, to leave my mother and I behind in order to obtain a visa that would allow us to emigrate. German Jewish refugees who attempted to flee the Nazi racial laws were not freely given permission to enter the United States for, in the 1930s, there was a strict quota system. One had to face America's formidable system of immigration laws. Applicants required an American sponsor willing to sign an affidavit of financial support promising the immigrant would not become a public charge and was of good health. In addition, one was required to have a job waiting as well as a place to live. This my father accomplished, and he rescued my mother and their eighteen-month-old toddler: myself. If he had not succeeded, my mother and I could not have survived.

More than seventy years later, in September 2010, I took another equally momentous sea voyage. I was one of seven Jewish passengers who, along with two journalists, set sail across the Mediterranean on a tiny catamaran. We were headed for the shores of Gaza in an attempt to break the siege and express solidarity as Jews against the suffering of Palestinians. The feeling as we sailed across the Mediterranean was one of joyful expectation. I did not imagine that Israeli warships would storm our vessel and that armed commandos would drag us to Ashdod prison to cruelly abort our mission of solidarity and hope. I could not imagine I would be deported from Israel and told I could not return for ten years.

In 1945, when the war against the Nazis ended, I was ten years old and lived with my parents in Jamaica, New York. Throughout my childhood and well into adulthood, I pushed the whole issue of the corruption of Germany by the Nazis to a deeply hidden place, unwilling and unable to identify myself as a German Jew. I was lost. Instead, I assumed my roles as a "good" daughter and a "good" American. Prior to leaving Germany, my family had been well-assimilated into German society as secular, non-religious Jews, like many German Jews who left Germany in the mid- to late 1930s. Being Jewish as a form of organized religion meant nothing to me. As I grew older, I haphazardly identified as a "cultural" Jew. In this way, I could hold on to some vestige of Jewish identification. When I married, politics became my religion, and I continued to bury my identification as a German Jew to a dark place within me, still left unexamined.

Years later, well into my fifties, I made numerous visits to relatives in Israel, refugees also from Germany who supported Israeli politics and lived comfortably. It was then I became aware of another aspect of Israel, a truly disturbing revelation for I, like so many Jews in the world, had idealized this land that I believed was created as a "beacon of light," a safe haven and land of compassion where refugees everywhere would be welcome. I look back and realize how idealistic was this image I had dreamed about and how naïve. Yet in my heart, I too had longed for a safe homeland.

This life-altering experience came to light when I met a first cousin of my father, who became my mentor and role model as both a critic and a lover of Israel. Hans Lebrecht, a former human rights activist and journalist, opened my eyes to a different Israel that for me was profoundly troubling. I had not been aware until then of Israel's insatiable hunger for land, or the racism I observed toward Palestinians, Sephardic Jews, Bedouins, and later, African asylum-seekers looking for work and political freedom. Awoken by Hans from my dream of a democratic, safe Israel, my love for the country had become tainted. How could Israel have built socialist-style communal living on someone else's land? It did not make sense. I grew agitated and heard half-remembered echoes of coarse shouts that I had suppressed for years: *"Refugees, reviled Jews who must be cleansed out of Germany and the rest of Europe!"* or, as heard from a neighbor in our family apartment in Jamaica, Queens, *"Those dirty Jews upstairs should have been killed by Hitler!"*

I wanted to love Israel, where I had felt safe, free, and happy to be Jewish. I loved the kibbutzim—the spirit of collective socialism and the pride of the people—as well as the beauty of the country. However, my identification as a refugee became a driving force in my empathy with the victimization and struggle of Palestinians; 700,000 Palestinians were thrown out in 1948, and those who have not died remain as homeless refugees. Remaining Palestinians live under a brutal occupation in the West Bank and Gaza. I am a witness. It has been a painful soul-searching journey for me to recognize and understand Israel as an oppressor nation. In addition, my curiosity concerning victims who had become victimizers also contributed to the birth of this book.

I ache for Israel, for its path of blind destruction that continues after five decades and three generations following its birth in 1948 to become an apartheid state separated by a nine-foot-high, 403-mile-long wall to keep out the "enemy." I am haunted by the question, after forty-eight years of apartheid, how can the occupation be ended? There is a sign in Hebron, "There is no Palestine and there never will be."

How is it possible that Jews, who themselves and their ancestors before them have been victims of the worst nightmare of the Final Solution, can turn away in blind denial? How can we forget the children, born into hate, living still in crowded camps that are breeding grounds for endless violence and conflict? It is all so familiar.

In 2010–2011, it was difficult to observe the demonization of Judge Richard Goldstone, a jurist and proud South-African Jew who set out to investigate international human rights violations during Operation Cast Lead in Gaza. He concluded that both Israel and Hamas had committed war crimes. Here was an opportunity to reflect and discuss, to have debates, and to engage in further investigations on both sides. But his report was squelched for the most part by Israel and the United States. He was ridiculed and humiliated as "a self-hating Jew," when nothing could be further from the truth.

It is a complicated question, how a hunted people have become hunters, how victims became victimizers. It may well be that it is the Israelis who feel the most persecuted; many of them still carry the weight of generations of hatred inflicted on them, and surely it has shaped the direction of their society. In my view, this hatred has been projected onto the "Other"—a Palestinian or a dissenting Jew.

In order to end the cycle of endless suffering for Jews and Palestinians, the Israeli powers-that-be can only benefit from self-examination, from honest and open dialogue including, of course, with the mistrusted "enemy." The goal must be mutual commonality and an end to demonizing the "Other." Left unexamined, the projection of hate onto those with other views and with diverse political persuasions succeeds only in perpetuating endless suffering and hatred that festers, destroys, and grows more virulent with each new generation.

I was carried out of Nazi Germany in the arms of my mother. This exodus, although not in my conscious memory, planted very early in my childhood seeds of rootlessness and feelings of a profound disconnect. So alone and apart was I, altogether different and awkward, yet not able to grasp the reasons for my alienation. Remnants of the experience of having one's roots pulled up violently have remained with me always. Then, as a child growing up, I longed to be American and not German. For decades, I denied my background, ignoring it as well as my refugee relatives. This unwanted part of me remained buried for decades, an amorphous, unexamined connection to my German homeland. That I felt different was perhaps a prophetic sign, for one day I would overcome the wish to be rid of all that was German. I would, in fact, be hungry to know my German-Jewish self. In my earlier years, fragments of loss, death, and fragility played with my imagination in my dreams.

My father, an assimilated Jew, considered himself more German than Jewish. He told me the Zionist movement had little impact on his family and other wealthy German Jews who identified themselves as an integral part of German society. They could have been called German nationalists, for they loved their country. But with the establishment of the Nuremburg laws, non-Jewish Germans started to refer to German Jews as foreigners.

I have struggled to organize the sequence of my personal and political lives, which remain inextricably intertwined. To do so has required that I scrutinize my life unflinchingly in order to examine deeply personal traumas with openness and honesty.

I am thinking about one Saturday evening in April 1999. I walked to Varick Street in Greenwich Village, New York. I was going to see a movie, *Wind Horse*. Wind horses are mystical creatures on whose backs Tibetans send prayers to dead ancestor spirits. Among the prayers are hopes for freedom. *Wind Horse* was filmed in Tibet and smuggled out. I shall not forget images of a Buddhist nun, tortured and subsequently dying in the arms of her family. I speak of this for it is another cruel example of man's inhumanity to man, repression and destruction, the occupation of Tibetans by the Chinese. The film never showed up again after it closed a few days later.

Some months later at a poetry reading, I heard the despair of a Cambodian physician once imprisoned with his pregnant wife in the killing fields of the Khmer Rouge. His words sent chills through the large room; his voice, in part a high-pitched scream, told us of the birth of his twin daughters, pulled out of his wife's womb by two Khmer guards as she lay on the dirt ground. Not long after he held them both in his arms, he threw them into the Mekong River as he sang a song for their souls and hoped they had been laid to rest. Only he survived to tell the story of another Holocaust. I cannot put into words how this man's suffering is every man's suffering—and if we cannot fathom this, then surely humanity is lost.

As I walked down Canal Street that evening in 1999, I thought about the imminent anniversary of my father's suicide, a result of repression and oppression of a different sort: personal family dynamics.

My father, politically oppressed himself, in turn oppressed his family. My parents left a country they loved and where they had thrived. They had dreams of their own and lived a rich, fulfilled life until Hitler assumed power. Part of a large, well-connected family, they had been young, energetic, and hopeful. But there was a dark side as well, for shortly after the Nuremberg Laws were passed, my paternal grandmother committed suicide as did my maternal grandfather. Depression and vicious racist laws, the destruction of their homeland, as well as the forced uprooting of a once intact family, must be understood as a driving force for their suicides, which I have no doubt were statements of deep despair.

The dark shadows of my refugee experience, in combination with a difficult and lonely childhood, make clearer my passionate quest (much later in my adult life) to break down barriers and artificial boundaries and to foster understanding between people. As a child, my voice was silenced. There was little room for self-expression. There were rules to be followed, rigid codes of behavior; and I was a very "good" girl who followed rules. I look back and recognize how Germanic my parents and their rules were! I felt I had no choice but to obey. When Hitler became chancellor, much of the German population were "good" German followers of the Nazi edicts, and rules had to be obeyed meticulously. In truth, my father, a good German, behaved like a little dictator in his own home. I was criticized from an early age and learned to keep my mouth shut. I felt caged as a child, a bird struggling (but seldom daring) to fly, to be free, and to find my own voice.

I know now that I was ashamed of my German family. I could only receive Mommy's love when I was a "good" girl who became what my mother wanted me to be, an extension of herself. Any form of rebellion created anxiety in my mother and reinforced a perception of me as a "bad" girl. Later in a difficult marriage, I was an unprepared parent, lost and in search of myself. I once had three children. My eldest son, Philip, died of a drug overdose in 1996. His death brought me to an awareness of the impermanence of life. This book was also born from these experiences that helped to shape who I am today.

How did I find my voice after such a repressed childhood? What drove my decision, when I was in my seventies, to be a passenger on the Jewish Boat to Gaza? How is it that as a refugee from Nazi Germany, I have come to be a critic of Israel?

It is not beyond comprehension to understand the policies of the Israeli government in light of Jewish history under the Nazi pogroms. We know Jews have suffered and have been victims. Is it that mentality behind the walls Israel has built? Are they still "victims" of paranoia and fear? Nationalism revisited is now twisted into a parody of the Nazi credo, "Deutschland über alles," extolling Germany over all others, with only pure Germans as inhabitants. "Get rid of the undesirables who are beneath contempt!" I must not make such a comparison, you may say. Yet I know that I must, for I fear a Jewish State that belongs only to Jews is a dangerous road. Many older generation Jews, their own psychological work left undone, carry within them deep scars of the Nazi Holocaust that is imprinted and lives on in the form of guilt, victimhood, and what I consider an irrational fear of another Holocaust brought on by exploding anti-Semitism in the world. Dwell upon the following words I heard recently from a group of Jews who are strong supporters of Zionism and their political agenda: "Without Israel, there would not be a safe Jew in the world." Those fears have yet to be confronted within the context of Zionist racist ideology.

The cycle of paranoia and abuse is playing out its destructive course: this is how I understand Palestinians as the last victims of the Holocaust. It is painful to attempt to understand what drove the Zionist movement in Israel/Palestine over the last sixty-seven years to continue on its determined path to separate itself, to have a Jewish state acquired through brute force and occupation.

I have divided this book into two parts, though in truth, they are one. First there is a personal story, my life as it was, presenting the dark shadows that surrounded our refugee experience, my parents' unhappiness, fragile moments, secrets, and a difficult, lonely childhood. Then, beginning in my fifties, I traveled to remote corners of the world, in search of cultures unscathed by modernity, missionizing, or Western development. My travels showed me unique cultures and provided an amazing recognition of the similarities of all beings, despite external differences. Years later, I would find the same human connection with Palestinians in the squalid, rotten refugee camps of Gaza. Their faces haunt me.

Part Two begins with my first visits to Israel as a politically unengaged Jewish woman who fell in love with the country. I gradually awakened to political realities and the most difficult question that remains to be discussed freely, without fear of censure: how can apartheid and a Jewish State survive together under the name of a democratic Jewish State? This immense question ultimately informed my decision to be a passenger on the Jewish Boat to Gaza. It was after our failed attempt to break the siege of Gaza and my imprisonment that I had an opportunity to visit Frankfurt, the city of my birth. What I found there provided a new set of surprises.

The reflections and conclusions in this book were first born in a place of disquiet and fear. It has been difficult to find the courage to speak out against a system that, in my view, attempts to destroy the very fabric of what it means to be Jewish and a humanist. My deepest belief holds that peace can come only when Israel/Palestine are a unified country living under mutual democracy, with dignity and equal rights. I invite you to set sail with me here, on this journey of survival and conscience.

Lillian Rosengarten
July 2015

PART ONE

ONE

Germany and America

In 1932, a year before Hitler became chancellor, my father Fritz Lebrecht was introduced to my mother, the beautiful, shy Lilli Jacob, at the Frankfurt municipal swimming pool. He was instantly smitten. The pool would close to Jews by late 1934. The Reich's citizen law stated, "A citizen of the Reich is that subject only who is of German or kindred blood and who, through his conduct, shows that he is both desirous and fit to serve the German people and Reich faithfully." My father, the youngest child of a prosperous, cultured, German-Jewish family had roots in Ulm, his birthplace. A bon vivant and womanizer in his youth, he liked to boast of his escapades. How proud he was to repeat the stories of his youth to my sister Carol and I, and to my mother, who had heard it all before, as we sat around in the gray atmosphere of the supper table. My mood would lighten, a short reprieve from the usual tension and bickering. There was little room for self-expression in our strict and rule-bound household.

My father would often say to me, "Think before you speak," which gradually reduced me to silence. Our small semi-attached sterile house in Bayside, New York, contrasted with the wealthy, indulgent environment of my father's youth. Two armchairs and a Danish-style couch in the living room were covered in plastic to preserve the horrid furniture forever. My mother handled her anxieties by saving everything. Fritz's stories from his youth, so distant from my own childhood, were intriguing to me. He spoke with nostalgia of parties in the Lebrecht family villa while his parents were away. He and his older brother Otto, no more than eighteen and twenty, would pour bottle after bottle of champagne into the family bathtub for communal frolicking and seductions. His stories embarrassed me, and yet I saw another side of my father: carefree, indulged, handsome, and powerful.

My father received a PhD in organic chemistry at the prestigious Heidelberg University. He liked to boast that his distant cousin Albert Einstein lectured one of his classes. When he met my mother, he was twenty-six years old and the CEO of the Frankfurt division of Lebrecht Lederwerkes, founded by my great-grandfather, Gabriel Lebrecht. The firm manufactured some of the finest leather goods in Europe. My mother's parents, Minnie and Rudolf Jacob, lived in Frankfurt, where Lilli was born in 1906. Frankfurt would be the city of my birth as well. My mother's early life was modest in comparison to my father's, but it was of no consequence, for Lilli's charm and beauty endeared her easily into the Lebrecht family. My mother never attended university, as it was not a priority in the bourgeois circles of my maternal grandparents. Instead, she was sent to Paris to study the art of dressmaking. Lilli had been brought up strictly and was innocent to the ways of the world when she met my father. On April 5, 1933, my parents were married and took their honeymoon at the chic resort Baden-Baden. They spoke often of their life in Germany with nostalgia and longing for the time when the country was still a democracy, prior to Hitler being appointed chancellor in January 1933.

One week before the election promised for March 1933, the Reichstag (German Parliament) burned down. Historical accounts suggest that a deranged communist from Holland and some of Hermann Göring's storm troopers scorched the building. Hitler took political advantage and claimed this was a signal that communists would take over Germany by force. President Hindenburg, old and ill, had been an admirer of Hitler and known to fear communism. He played into Hitler's manipulations and granted him emergency power. Hitler seized the opportunity to ban communists and socialists from voting and to maintain "law and order." In addition, the new laws provided the "Brown Shirts" (the SA, precursor to the SS) permission to violently roam the streets to harass, beat, and murder those who opposed Hitler without interference.

On a beautiful evening in the fall of 1934, my parents decided to take an after-dinner stroll on Frankfurt's Feuerbach Strasse, the elegant neighborhood where they lived. The air was soft and caressed the beautiful linden trees my parents would speak of with nostalgia in my childhood years. Suddenly a group of young Brown Shirts jumped out from nowhere. Five men marched up to my parents while simultaneously clicking their heels. No more than eighteen years old, they had clean-shaven angel faces, hardly out of childhood but already indoctrinated with hate. High boots were laced over brown pants, Nazi flags pinned on brown caps and armbands in red, white, and black. One Brown Shirt stepped close to my father, stared into his face and lifted a finger to touch his nose. He laughed, circled around, and shouted, "Come see the Jew nose!" Face filled with contempt, he spewed hatred through his words while the others cursed and mocked. My father was dressed elegantly in a tailored suit, silk tie, expensive overcoat, and fine, black leather gloves. A small Florentine gold pin engraved with a diamond "L" was prominent on his tie. I would see it often as a child, as I had heard this story so many times from my father. My mother, then pregnant with me, was wearing a sable fur hat to match the collar and cuffs of her stylish coat. As I lay inside my mother, I surely became an unseen witness. Number two kicked, taunted, cursed, then punched my father in the face until he bled. The Brown Shirt angel faces in high spirits kicked him to the ground, taunted some more, and marched away. My mother, although physically unharmed, would live with anxiety throughout her life and, in her late years, be swept into a psychotic form of bipolar illness.

My father saw the writing on the wall. A realist, he had the courage to leave Germany. It would take him two years to get us out. High unemployment, despair, and fear had permeated German-Jewish society, where Hitler's strong rhetoric mesmerized a population. They heard and embraced big daddy's promises to lead them into prosperity.

There is a photograph in which I sit on the lap of my grandmother Minnie. I am about fourteen months old; her arms hold me, and she looks down at me. We are in Frankfurt. Germany was already under Nazi leadership. What was she thinking? Why was she

Lillian as a toddler with her family in Frankfurt.

alone? My parents to the right are strikingly beautiful; my mother's smile lights up her young face. My father leans into my mother; he does not smile, his face serious, intense. All three wear their wedding rings on the customary right hand. They are elegantly dressed. My aunt Melitta, next to her mother, does not smile. Her husband, my uncle Paul, sits erect, unsmiling. I wonder about their sad faces.

I had idealized this photo. Surrounded by a happy, intact family all together in Germany while nurtured in an environment of security and love. Sadness lurks behind the photo of the family with deep roots and a promising future. I believe my parents were deeply in love for the first few years of their marriage. The photo took on different meanings as I became aware of the trauma of Nazi Germany that tore families apart. Perhaps my aunt, never able to have children of her own, suffered even then. Decades later, she became mentally ill—involutional melancholia, as it was called in those days.

I became aware of this photo when I began to question how I had at one time been a part of a German-Jewish family still intact.

It was during the time I was invited by the mayor of Ulm to a reunion of German Jews who lived in Ulm and emigrated during the Nazification of Germany. It was the early 1990s; my parents had died, and I would represent the Fritz Lebrecht side of the family. My father's first cousin, Richard Lebrecht, now deceased, took me on a spectacular tour to show me our family villa and various graves, but sadly I never knew where my paternal grandparents, Gustave and Gisela, were buried. Perhaps the cemetery had been destroyed. This trip put me in touch with relatives I had not met before who had emigrated to Brazil, Chile, Israel, and parts of the United States. Present also were other beloved family members I had known, Hans and Tosca Lebrecht, her sister Esther Béjarano, and Hans and Tosca's daughter Margalith Pozniak, with whom I remain in close contact. Many I met during these important two weeks in Ulm, all of whom knew my father, have since died.

I shall not forget my visit to one of the first notorious camps in the outskirts of Ulm, Kuhberg detention center. It existed from November 1933 to July 1935, built for political prisoners who had resisted Hitler, socialists and communists. A ghastly place, one felt the ghosts of tortured souls and death reverberate throughout the cold stone rooms. My body weakened as tears took over, a burst of emotion set free where there were no words to speak. Kuhberg stands as a documentation center and remains shocking in its brutality.

There is a photo of my mother and my aunt Melitta sitting together at about age fifteen months. Dressed in matching white eyelet dresses, they appear completely innocent and charming. The good life in Germany was not expected to end. I stared at this photo of another time and wondered about the relationship between the rise of Nazism and the mental illness so prevalent in my family. The contrast between life in Germany and their anxious lives in New York created many problems for my parents, who struggled to adjust into a life of relative poverty.

My family led an affluent life in Germany. There was music and theater in their lives. My father spoke of family chamber music concerts, founded by his father, the grandfather I never knew. He was a violinist, so music was an integral part of their lives. My paternal aunt Grete became a pianist, and I would also one day study piano. They lived a life of privilege in pre-Nazi Germany and were deeply attached to their German nationality. As assimilated Jews, religion played a minor role. What might my life have been like in a Germany without Nazism? I identify with refugees who too were torn from their roots, displaced and disoriented.

When my father landed in New York, he quickly worked to secure visas for my mother and me. The U.S. Department of Immigration held our fate in its hands, as clearly not everyone received permission to enter. Visas were granted based on proof of a sponsor. His sponsor, the owner of a small leather export/import business, appointed Fritz as a middle manager, a position that led nowhere. He stayed for thirty years, unable to let himself embrace his own professional yearnings. He found our first apartment on Steinway Street in Astoria, Queens. Nearly penniless, for they could take only some pieces of furniture but not any money, my parents were severed from their beloved Germany, friends, family, and affluence. Settling in New York with their little daughter, they found themselves adrift in a sea of strangers, unmoored from their station in life and terribly unhappy. They brought with them a darkness that became for me a personal symbol of the nightmare of Hitler's Germany. They longed for the world they had left.

My parents found it difficult to adjust to American ways, and this left its mark. I never knew where I belonged. I was raised in a strict Germanic household and spoke German at home, yet attended an American public school. I was shy, an outsider, never like the other girls who seemed to be so sure of themselves, with beautiful outfits they had bought in stores. I was certainly not popular and wore the clothes my mother made for me on her old Singer sewing machine. All I wanted was to be like the others. Instead I had poor self-esteem and felt ashamed of my background as a German Jew.

My father's dream of academia, to teach chemistry and do research, was never realized. My mother held him back. Fearful of losing everything again, she obsessively scrimped and saved while managing every penny my father brought home. Most important for her was the steady salary my father received. Risks were something she could not tolerate. I wish Fritz could have spoken up to assert his own needs and take a stand. Instead, he gave in to my mother and pushed away his own drive and ambition.

Because she could not spend money, my mother never bought anything for herself. Instead she wore the outdated German clothes I hated to the point of embarrassment. It used to bother me to hear her thick German accent and the way she mixed up German with her broken English: "Ach das ist so schlimm (bad)." I wanted my mother to be like other moms, to dress like them and have fun. I hid from everything German. I didn't like Germans very much and my mother embarrassed me; she herself was shy and awkward. She was also strict and controlling. I recall our trips to Best and Company where I was forced to have my hair cut. So many times I pleaded with her, for I hated how I looked after the scissors did their damage.

Yet, I did admire many things about her. She could be full of energy and drive. In her fifties, she became a certified yoga instructor and Red Cross swim teacher. She was proud of her accomplishments, but I rarely acknowledged her success and could not be excited for her. I wish I had felt more connected, listened to her stories to tell to my own children and grandchildren. My mother could be shy or bold, distant or needy. She could be brutally critical or seductively charming. I wanted her and was also physically repelled. I could rarely allow myself to feel her warmth. When she attempted to get close, she seemed to want all of me, to need me too much. Yet I wanted her love and to be close to her.

A memory is etched; I as a little child, age three, locked in a room by my mother, left alone to scream inconsolably. I must have been a bad girl. There had been no soothing, only silence. In those early years, my mother had grown increasingly anxious. She would lament, "Gisela, if I had stayed in Germany, I could have been a successful designer." She would wring her hands and frown; the tension of her scrunched-up forehead would accent the tightness around her mouth. She picked at her lips in a nervous manner. Then, she would invariably walk away. She cast her darkness on our family. Yet my mother also found creative ways to ease our financial struggles. She raised me frugally, without "things," so I grew up modestly. Later, when I married a wealthy man, I had little interest in his monetary worth.

My mother taught herself to string pearls. With her charm and a lot of nerve, another side of her emerged as she solicited expensive jewelers in the city, such as Van Cleef & Arpels, De Pinna, and Bergdorf Goodman, who became her clients. At night I watched them, my father with a Lucky Strike balanced at the edge of his mouth, ashes about to drop, and my mother determined to teach him the fine art of pearl stringing. I have no idea how she had learned it herself. There they sat, working together. Two goose-neck lamps on either end of the table highlighted the pearls, clasps, and nylon string, all laid out on the stringing boards. Endless patience and concentration, together with perseverance, brought in business for ten years. Intensely absorbed, with not a word spoken, I watched my mother and father laboriously knot each pearl onto the string. The finest pearls, sometimes owned by famous people, were always knotted, whereas cheap pearls required no knots. Every Tuesday, my mother dressed up in her wool suit, a small hat flirtatiously worn over her dark brown, thick, pageboy hairdo. She would rave about her hairdresser, Larry Matthews, who trimmed her hair and only charged two dollars. On Tuesdays in the fancy stores, she would introduce herself as a Parisian designer, and she pulled it off.

My father brought my grandmother Minnie out of Germany to live with us when I was three years old, soon after we arrived in New York. (Looking back, it was amazing he managed it.) She was just sixty-one when she arrived. I never found out in her lifetime why she came without my grandfather Rudolf. His name rarely came up and I did not ask. I thought of her as alone, never with a husband. It was as if Rudolf never existed. She was the only grandparent I knew, and I loved her gentle ways, her artistic being, her watercolors, her cooking. My Omi died of congestive heart failure when she was seventy-three in her room next to mine. I was fourteen and

Lillian and her mother.

could hear her moan. Perhaps the bedsores hurt, or she felt alone and frightened. My mother and aunt Melitta nursed her until the end. I was not allowed to enter her room or attend her funeral, so I never had the chance to say goodbye. My feelings were disregarded. Now I understand it was the German way, at least within our family, to keep everything hidden, secret. Why couldn't I simply have opened the door to her room, held her close in my arms, and told her how much I loved her? Why did they keep her from me? Why did I keep myself from her? I was a "good" girl who dared not speak up, and I was incapable of defiance.

There was a secret I did not learn about until I was an adult, long after my Omi's death. My grandfather Rudolf owned a dry goods store at #5 Kaiserstrasse, an elegant neighborhood in Frankfurt am Main. He traveled annually to Paris to order fine material for his store. This material would be turned into stylish dresses for wealthy Frankfurt clientele. On April 1, 1933, one week after Hitler became chancellor, Joseph Goebbels, the Nazi propaganda minister, gave

Nazi storm troopers posting signs on a Berlin store with the words: "Deutsche! Wehrt Euch! Kauft nicht bei Juden!" ("Germans! Defend yourselves! Do not buy from Jews!"). From the German Federal Archive.

a speech in Berlin urging Germans to boycott Jewish-owned businesses. Nazi storm troopers blocked the entrances to Jewish stores. Their signs read, "Germans, defend yourselves against the Jewish atrocity propaganda; buy only at German shops!" In the period between March and October 1933, 536 Jewish business enterprises in Frankfurt were closed. My grandfather Rudolf hung himself in his store after the Nazi decree to close down his shop. I suspect he may have suffered from depression, as both his daughters became bipolar in their later life. But I cannot be certain that it was not simply the Nazi decree to close his store that led to his demise. It haunts me to know that my Omi carried this grief alone. I cannot imagine how she lived with this secret. I suppose I never really knew her. Decades later, I visited Frankfurt and saw my grandfather's store on Kaiserstrasse #5, the apartment where he and my grandmother had lived in the elegant west end section, and his lonely grave in the old Jewish cemetery.

My sister, Carol, was born in 1941. Strangely, she always seemed more German than me, for she had lived with my parents all her life and adopted many of their mannerisms as well as their way of speaking. I resented my sister, who appeared out of nowhere when I was six years old. My parents and grandmother had forgotten to tell me I was to have a baby sister or brother. I actually remember asking my mother, late into her pregnancy, why she had become so fat. I can still see the bedroom where I stood looking at my mother, and I will never forget her response: "I am eating too much spinach." How unrelated she was to me at age six, how crazy this deception! One day my mother was gone, and when she returned to the apartment with my father, she was holding my infant sister in her arms. Who was this intruder? I did not want her there. What a sad way to meet one's only sister.

Carol was sickly and asthmatic from the beginning. Her birth should have been joyful for surely it symbolized our survival. Carol's earliest years coincided with the Final Solution: crematoriums that burned day and night, gassed flesh turned to ashes as millions of souls were released through smoke stacks that stank from the ninth circle of hell, the Nazi death camps. (Yet how much did I know of what was happening in Europe? Although my father was an avid reader who read *Aufbau* every week to keep up with German life, news of his friends, births, and deaths, he did not speak of death camps. As a child, I do not recall hearing about the Holocaust. There were many secrets in our family. Perhaps I do not remember. Surely my parents knew, for my father rescued many members of our family and brought them out of Germany.)

How sad that I never felt the spirit of celebration around Carol's birth. Despite my parents instructing me from an early age to "always take care of your sister," I bent over backward to completely disregard their wish. I was unable to feel empathy for my sister, whose role had been designated as a target for my parent's frustrated selves. Carol was easy prey, for she was a vulnerable and fearful child. My critical and controlling parents would need her to contain and sustain their troubled marriage.

43

Throughout their life, Carol was the glue that held my parents together. As long as they could scapegoat Carol, they were able to turn away from their own problems. The climate in our household made it difficult for my sister and I to form a nurturing relationship with each other. I have come to know now that Carol also missed not having a sister she could trust to be on her side. I tried in my later years to overcome the alienation between us, yet still find ways to remain distant. When she was in her twenties, I tried to help Carol move out of the house; she had been unable to separate from our parents to make a life for herself. It was 1964 and I was by then married with three small children. Carol had completed a nursing degree at a local community college, but her attempt to move away was short-lived. She developed eczema on her hands, making it impossible for her to work, and this ultimately forced her back to our parents' house. Carol's asthma symbolized for me the tightness and constriction of her life and the repression in the household. My parents failed to help her make the transition to independence. Sadly, she remained living with them as their caregiver until their deaths. I recognize now my need to stay away, to separate myself for my own survival. I cannot, however, escape the whispers of guilt for having left the burden of my parents to my sister.

I recall the climate in our household during my teen years. Our house was easily recognized, the only one on the block with no Christmas lights. Hanukkah was our annual holiday, but it lacked a true religious tradition with the exception of our one and only song, "Rock of Ages." The few moments before we opened our presents as we stood around a candlelit dining room table, I could feel something Jewish, a connection of sorts, however fragile. It was a reminder that we were indeed Jews. My father used to say we were German and assimilated. Many German Jews felt this way.

My mother did try to instill in me some form of a Jewish religion, but her ineffectual attempts proved humiliating. She insisted that we, my mother and I, sneak into the High Holiday services at Temple Israel every year. Why Carol was not with us, I will never know. Imagine what it was like for me, a reluctant participant, while my mother momentarily pretended we were members as we slid into balcony seats for the High Holiday services. Dressing in our finest meant being dressed in my German handmade clothes and a coat from Klein's bargain basement. Once seated, for a few moments it seemed we were safe. I slouched down and hoped to disappear. We were always caught and led out the door. I felt humiliated. I suppose we were too poor to pay or my mother believed Jewish refugees should not pay. In truth, only paying members were allowed in on the High Holidays.

My father, on the other hand, would not step foot inside a synagogue. He was an atheist, his loyalties more German than Jewish. I have wondered whether he could have been a member of the Nazi Party had he not been a Jew because of his strong nationalistic identification. I hope I am wrong, and that if we had discussed this, my father would have vehemently denied the possibility. Another side of him identified with socialism and class equality. Years later, he was a proud American. He expressed a lifelong gratitude to America, the country that took us in.

My parents' marriage, based on an initial strong physical attraction, proved intellectually frustrating for my father, and he humiliated my mother more than once. He made fun of her annual "bursts of religion." I also would have none of it and found no solace in religion. Yet I remember well two German childhood prayers my father taught me. Now I believe they were prayers for Christian children. I would say one or the other before I fell asleep comforted by both my mother and father as they stood close to me. I was ten or perhaps younger. I felt loved during these moments of innocence in childhood, and now I am filled with sadness for the innocence lost.

Mude bin ich, geh zu Ruh
Schliesse beide euglein zu
Vater lass die augen dein
Uber meinen bettchen sein
I am tired, go to sleep
Close both my little eyes.

Father, let your eyes
Be over my little bed.

Ich bin klein
Mein hertz ist rein
Soll niemand drin wohnen
Als Gott nur allein.
I am little;
My heart is pure.
No one shall live there
Except God alone.

I am sure there were many times I felt happy. I must remember that no matter what difficulties have confronted me, I am also capable of great joy. I recall days I stayed home from school when I was sick. Once I had mumps and then chicken pox, the illnesses of childhood in the 1940s. I remember a small radio next to my bed with stations called WEAF, WOR, and WJC. I can still feel my happiness when my mother or grandmother made me breakfast and lunch that I would eat as I listened to *My True Story* at 10 a.m. or the soap operas later in the day. I would imagine elaborate scenes, rich in detail, coming out of the radio. I loved the characters in the stories: Stella Dallas, My Gal Sunday Helen Trent, Lorenzo Jones and his wife Belle. I even listened to Kate Smith and Arthur Godfrey; both, I learned later in life, were arch-conservatives. None of it mattered then. When I needed some medicine and did not want to take it, my father would knock on my door in the evening after he returned home. He would pretend to be Dr. Neuhaus, our family doctor, also a refugee, whom I detested. I believed the hated doctor would enter my room if I refused to take the medicine. And so it went, my parents were involved, and I felt their love during those special times.

I remember a happy day my parents took me to my first movie at Radio City Music Hall. I must have been around ten or eleven. I had no idea what a movie looked like. I asked my parents, while the Rockettes were dancing, "Is this the movie?" We saw *Wintertime*, and I was in heaven that day.

My joy was often wrapped in emotional pain, for both lived together side by side. Etched deeply in my memory was a time at age five when my parents left me on a swing in a children's home (*kinderheim*) to take a hiking vacation in the White Mountains. They simply disappeared without telling me they would once again return.

I was nine years old the day I was naturalized in 1944. I rid myself of my German name Gisela and chose Lillian. By chance I had heard someone say the name Lillian in the line while I waited. This would be my American name. I had been named after my paternal grandmother, Gisela. I never knew her for she had committed suicide before I was conceived. Her death was one more family secret; no one spoke of suicide. I have been drawn to the spirit of my grandmother throughout my life. Without her knowledge, she has kept me close to my roots, and I have felt myself as a part of her. I had a dream as a young woman in which she appeared lifelike and spoke to me:

It was a terrible time in Germany, my dear, for Hitler was taking power. Of course we believed we would not be touched by the dark clouds that hovered over us. We saw ourselves as an educated elite of Germany, creative, productive, and wealthy. Over generations we had assimilated into the society, well-insulated and secure as 'good Germans.' I did, however, have a premonition that you and I would never know one another. This, dear Gisela, is a sad truth of my life. I wanted to be a grandmother to hand down my legacy to you. You and I were destined to be alike in our sensibilities, our love of nature, our gentle being as well as our love for music. I too played Bach and Mozart on the piano. I left Fritz my unabridged urtext four-hand Mozart, Handel, Schumann, and Schubert. Did you play this music with your father? Did he pass the music down to you? Do you still have it? Dear one, I want to tell you a secret. I suffered for some years from depression and kept it to myself. Depression was not something one spoke about. One day, during the darkest hours of my life, I took a fateful plunge to my death. Perhaps it was the rise of Hitler, our loss of personal power as our beloved Germany morphed into his cruel and vile racial laws, which deepened my depression and made living intolerable. Perhaps it was that depression was not spoken about. This ancestral secret, dear one, I offer to you as a gift of light. Let the secret no longer remain buried. Do not be afraid to show yourself, my darling granddaughter. Stand always with pride in the light.

My grandmother Gisela had been my spiritual connection to my German roots. My own mother, Lilli, was distant. I did not know then how much she needed me to conform, to be like her. Perhaps I imagined that choosing my new name would bring me closer to her for then we could both be "Lilli."

As we stood in the long line awaiting our citizenship test, my father coached me. He needed to make sure I would not say anything that could hurt our chances of becoming citizens. I can remember to this day how he told me not to forget to tell the examiners that Hitler was a terrible man, that he was our enemy. Of course I knew that already and did not need to be reminded. I was nine and knew why I was there. My mother insisted I stay in line and yanked me back whenever I wandered off. She hovered close while I looked up at my father's face, his warm brown eyes, a Lucky Strike between his lips. I loved him very much. Tall and thin, he wore his straight brown hair parted on the right side and was dressed in a familiar blue striped suit with a white handkerchief in the breast pocket. My mother wore a light green wool suit, her ever-present little blue brooch pinned to the collar of her embroidered white blouse. The suits, once elegant, were worn and dated. By the end of the day, I was naturalized. We were citizens. Now, I was both German and American.

When I was ten, my best friend and worst enemy, Joyce Eriksson, lived across the street. She was a two-faced friend, and I could never be sure when she would turn on me. She either liked me or hated me. Because I was afraid of her, she wielded a lot of power. She would make fun of me and turn the girls in the neighborhood against me. That our family was one of only two Jewish families on the block fed into frequent moments of alienation and discomfort with the other kids in the neighborhood. Surely my mother's overprotectiveness did not help and contributed to my feeling different. She kept me tightly under her ever-watchful eyes. Her anxious ways rubbed off on me and added to my insecurity. I would feel angry and embarrassed when she would not allow me go to a neighborhood movie on a weekend with the other kids. My mother had no idea how to help me fit in. Her strict ways further alienated me in my awkwardness. She held on so tightly, and this kept me from just having fun like a normal kid. Instead I became her "good girl," albeit not happy and carefree. After dinner during warm weather, the street below the two-family house where we lived on the second floor was alive. The neighborhood kids loved to hang out on one of our stoops. Those were fun times cut short when my mother called from the window to announce it was time to come up. No one else's mother did that. I felt different and embarrassed. Why did she have to stop me from life?

When Joyce wanted to be my friend, I was happy. One day on my way home from school, I spotted Joyce and two of her friends. As they approached me, Joyce shouted, "The Jews killed Christ, Christ Killer!" The others joined in, "Christ Killer, you killed Christ." I walked faster as their taunts continued. I turned to them and yelled back, "No they didn't!" I was in tears and wanted only to be home. I didn't understand what I had to do with killing Christ anyway. Why did people have to blame the Jews? I was afraid but did not quite realize it was anti-Semitism that had so unnerved me. At the supper table, I asked my father why people said the Jews killed Christ. "Who told you this, Gisela?" His face white, he lit a Lucky Strike. "It is completely untrue. Jesus himself was a Jew, murdered by the Romans." I watched my father mindlessly flick ash onto the table. Silence. My father turned to my mother and reached for her hand. She pulled back, unable to offer comfort. Then from someplace far, my father spoke, "Mein Gott Lilli, hier ist dasselbe; the same thing is going on in America. We cannot get away."

Throughout the years, my father became frustrated and increasingly angry toward my mother, but he never could express himself directly. He would be critical or make a joke to undermine her.

I would say he was passive-aggressive. He must have resented my mother for holding him back professionally. With his PhD in chemistry, my father, an intellectual, could not let himself pursue the academic and research life he had spoken about with such regret. A wild fury must have lodged in the depth of his being that embittered him and fueled his brief periods of depression. Fortunately, he would rebound quickly and return to a self that combined charm, frustration, anger, and self-deprecation. I wonder if the women in his life—myself, Carol, and my mother—might have lived happier lives if my father had found the courage to fulfill his dreams. My mother, riddled with anxiety as she grew older, became the recipient of his criticism, as did we. Our exodus from Germany burdened my father, who always believed he was held back by my mother's exaggerated fears. Because my father could not stand up for what he needed, he put my mother's fears in front of his own professional needs. As a lover of books and ideas, he resented her lack of intellect. The marriage had been a poor fit.

I learned to hide my spontaneity and much of my own creativity. I was angry with my parents for attempting to hold me in their world for so long. Poor grades, painful shyness, and a lack of confidence made my high school years forgettable. Somehow I knew I had to leave that house as soon as possible after graduation. Yet, my parents had shown extraordinary courage and bravery. Their grandeur was their awareness of the oncoming nightmare of Hitler's war against Jews, Gypsies, disabled folks, homosexuals, and dissenters—those who raised their voices against the madness around them.

Throughout my teens, my father's need to control grew stronger, as did my mother's anxiety. She continued to scrimp, and my father, who could be so charming in the company of others, continued to criticize. I did not feel good about myself or my emerging sexuality. I had no dates, felt like a wallflower, and could not focus enough to get decent grades. To make matters worse, my father could not stand up to Lilli, which further enraged him. The times when my mother was able to relax her tight grip, when she attempted to venture out of her fear and meet the world on its own terms, my father found a way to stamp her out, to undermine or criticize. He was critical of her yoga practice. She eventually had a following of students. My father never seemed to value her strengths and her accomplishments. He treated her like a child, placating her instead of recognizing her as a woman who had mastered a career and had accomplished much against many odds. Perhaps because of my father's contempt, I too failed to recognize her accomplishments, although she longed for recognition from us.

I did not do well enough in high school to get into college, and my parents never encouraged me. A wealthy German friend of my parents, Julius Steiner, was a benefactor to Mount Sinai Hospital. When I applied to the School of Nursing, he spoke on my behalf because my grades were too poor for me to be accepted on my own. This was my entrance into a new world that would provide me with a profession. It was a key to freedom and my entrée into a road of self-discovery. In 1953, I moved out of the house and pushed the German Jewish refugee underground.

TWO
Away from Home

How fortunate that I found the strength to leave my parents! When I received a letter inviting me to interview at the School of Nursing, I initially felt anxious. However on the day itself, when I sat in the large office opposite Minnie Struthers, the assistant director of nursing, I noticed kindness in her face. I was impressed with her starched, spotless white uniform, the Mount Sinai cap sitting proudly atop her silver hair. I was seventeen and about to step into a new life. I still recall her words to me: "You have potential, but you will have to work very hard." I was thrilled to know I had been accepted. The three rigorous years I spent in the nursing program were a wonderful time in my life. I became a part of the Mount Sinai Hospital community as well as one of ten struggling nursing students in my class of February 1956.

A miraculous door had been opened that changed my life. When I graduated, I noticed a glimpse of my intelligence and sensitivity. I had done very well and did not have a more difficult time than anyone else in training, an important milestone for me. I became a New York registered professional nurse and was liberated. I loved my work as head nurse of Ward K, where I taught student nurses and took charge of a forty-bed women's medical unit. Eventually, I moved out of the nurses' dormitory and found an apartment, which I shared with Rose, a Sinai friend. Imagine a one-bedroom apartment on East 93rd off Lexington. It's hard to believe our rent was $150, utilities included and split between us. I did not have to rely on anyone to support me. I was free!

I first met Frank, the man I would marry, in the lobby of Carnegie Hall on February 18, 1959. That afternoon, my love of music had brought me to the Boston Symphony. I had borrowed Rose's dress, as it accented my five-foot-six slender frame and small, high breasts. Although I liked my wild, dark, unruly hair, I was self-conscious.

When I was seven, my mother had said to me, "I think I am not your mother, Gisela. You must be a stepchild for no one in our family has curls." She had confused me with her words, repeating more than once that I was not her child. She was unaware that, in part, I believed her.

As I approached the box office at Carnegie Hall, a tall, dark-haired, well-dressed man waved a ticket in the air. "Do you need a ticket?" He sprinted toward me in a fit of energy and explained it was a great seat, for only six dollars. "That's too much money," I said, and I meant it. Six dollars was too expensive for me. He sold it to me for three and I followed him up the stairs to the family box. The greeting I received, "Welcome to the family for the afternoon," could not have been more prophetic. I was shown to the front of the box and took a seat. Only once did I turn around to notice the tall stranger, his eyes fixed on me.

That was how it began. I was naïve, unformed, and completely vulnerable. After the concert, Frank asked me to join him for a drink, and we walked a few blocks to the Oak Room of the Plaza Hotel. I had no idea what to make of this man who showed such an interest in me. I learned he was thirty-one and was completing a doctorate at Columbia University in modern postwar Italian literature and politics. He taught Dante as an adjunct professor. I was impressed and intimidated, shy and relieved that he did most of the talking. Never had I met anyone so intellectual. I felt inferior. We were different not only in age, but also in our life experience. Frank had been married and divorced. He had traveled and studied in Italy for several years.

Frank's world of intellect and privilege was unfamiliar and made my head spin. It soon became clear that Frank's family was rich. They had two homes, one in Hewlett Harbor, a wealthy Jewish enclave of the Five Towns on the south shore of Long Island, and the other a duplex apartment in Gramercy Park. They employed a live-in couple and rode in a chauffeured Bentley. I had no interest in their wealth; it was more important that they liked me. Despite their former position in Germany, my parents' life was worlds apart from that of Frank's parents. I was completely seduced by his attention, the sophistication of his world, his life experience and maturity. I did not know then how Frank's alcoholism would eventually become a destructive force in our marriage.

My parents met Frank briefly when he picked me up for a date in Bayside. On occasion, I would spend a weekend with them. To my surprise, both my parents were completely taken with Frank. He appeared refined and well-spoken, attributes that impressed them. Frank held the door as I stepped into his car on that first date. He looked me over and smiled. "You look beautiful," he said. Beautiful? Was he speaking to me? I had heard others say I was pretty or unusual-looking, but I never thought of myself as beautiful. Frankly, I had no idea how I looked.

At a party given by one of his students who lived in Great Neck, Long Island, we parked ourselves on a corner couch and talked. Every now and then, Frank would get up to socialize briefly and then sit down again with a fresh drink in his hand. We were absorbed for hours. He asked whether I would come back with him to his apartment. I accepted with no hesitation. I am sure I was seduced by his attention and the novelty of this experience. Frank's apartment on Ninth Street off Fifth Avenue had a quiet, elegant feel. Bookshelves lined the walls, some small antiques here and there, nothing overdone and certainly not shabby. He poured himself a cognac and made a cup of tea for me.

He put on a record, Prokofieff's Fifth Symphony, and sat down next to me on the couch in front of a small fireplace. I was moved when I noticed his tears. It touched me that this man could show his emotions so freely, could be so affected by music. We sat and then his lips were on mine. I was taken by surprise. I did not quite know what I was doing there. My response was completely physical and without thought. My body responded to Frank's lovemaking while completely detached from my emotions and thoughts, a mind-body disconnect, so to speak. I was lonely, flattered, and unprepared for what was to come.

As our mouths touched, my hunger took me by surprise. I felt a slow tingle between my legs, the private place wet and eager. Detached from thoughts, my body took over. Perhaps that was what made it so good. I was consumed with desire. There was no emotional connection yet. I was swept into flight. His desire for me ceased to matter, and even he ceased to matter as I took off. On his big bed, he entered me and as his sex filled my body, I was lifted high, higher, then crashed in complete surrender. Afterward, I lay in Frank's arms until morning. It was then our son Philip was conceived.

Some weeks later I was frantic. I had missed my period. I was pregnant, unmarried, and not in love. How could I have let this happen? Could I simply say I was naïve? It didn't occur to me that Frank was also responsible. Why didn't he use protection? I never questioned it. I stood at the sidelines without truly entering my life or taking on the responsibility of my actions. The passivity I assumed during that time of my life would backfire, causing unhappiness and deep dissatisfaction, but I knew no other way. Scared and completely unprepared for motherhood, I became frantic. Abortion, although illegal, was something I could have arranged through my medical contacts. It never even entered my consciousness.

I had to tell Frank. Over supper at Rocco's in Greenwich Village, I blurted out, "Frank, I'm pregnant." The immediate joy in his face came as a surprise. His arms reached toward me and he took hold of my hands. I had not been aware of the depth of his feelings. "My darling girl, how absolutely marvelous." His words momentarily swept me into his excitement. He wanted to marry me. I felt shame. In the 1950s, couples were supposed to be married before a child was conceived. We were nearly strangers, having met only a few months before. I struggled to sort through my feelings, my unplanned pregnancy, and how quickly my life had turned upside down. I was miserable.

One evening, I broke down to my roommate, Rose. I spoke of my unhappiness, my fears and confusion, and she offered me an insight. Her simple and straightforward response was completely unexpected. "Sometimes Lillian, the happiness you are searching for is right there in front of you and you don't even notice it." Although the prospect of happiness had not occurred to me, pregnancy was a reason to get married. It was the only thing to do, and that was why I accepted Frank's marriage proposal.

I had to go to Bayside to tell my parents about the baby. I was anxious and afraid that my parents would be critical, shocked, or disappointed. We sat down for the usual great German dinner my father had prepared for us. I had no appetite, and the rumblings in my stomach signaled distress.

Over tea, I said, "I'm going to have a baby. Frank and I will get married." *God,* I thought, *I feel awful.*

My parents responded with complete joy and excitement. I could hardly believe it. My body relaxed and I too began to smile. We hugged. Carol, then seventeen, came over and wrapped her arms around me. In my wildest dreams, I would not have anticipated this response. My mother poured tea and my father walked over to his cabinet and took out a bottle of Schnapps.

"Let's toast." he said. "Our first grandchild, Gisela. This is wonderful." He smiled at my mother, who also looked happy. It was a warm moment.

Frank's parents accepted me easily into the family. They were thrilled and fawned over me. They had hoped Frank would remarry, settle down. They were excited to become grandparents, the first of six. Phil was special from the moment he was announced. Everything swirled around me so fast, and I could not catch up. I was swept into a completely new lifestyle. That I had become financially liberated as a result of marriage barely impacted me; it simply didn't seem to matter. Despite having been born into wealth, Frank had developed a strong social conscience and believed in a more equitable system in which societies were not divided between rich and poor. He wanted poverty to be eradicated and wrote about principles of social justice. He opened a new world of ideas to me.

We married at City Hall on April 27, 1959. It was a quick, mechanical ceremony with little emotion. We still hardly knew one another. I didn't understand how I came to be married there that Tuesday morning with so little fanfare. I had not even involved myself in planning my own wedding. It all just "happened." How odd to be married without parents, friends, or love. I had few dreams then, only the dreams of others. I was naïve and knew that I was pregnant. It seemed the right thing to do, to marry the father. I hardly had opinions but latched onto the opinions of others. I was naïve and Frank was worldly. This I knew.

Rose was our witness as I carried the shame of my pregnancy within me. Afterward, Frank left to teach his Tuesday class at Adelphi College. Rose and I went to see the film *Imitation of Life.*

I moved out of my apartment and began life with Frank. What feels so strange now is to acknowledge how I actually believed I could be anything my husband wanted me to be: a pretzel shaped by someone else, malleable and without a mind of my own. This may have been the role of some women prior to the women's movement in the 1970s. Perhaps I simply use that as an excuse to justify how completely unformed I was in my early twenties. In some respects, I recognize now a strong possibility my marriage had somehow mirrored that of my parents. I too was charming and good-looking but had few opinions of my own. I, like my mother, married a wealthy intellectual. To acknowledge this parallel is a revelation to me now. Perhaps my relationship with Frank in those early years was not only shaped by a strict upbringing but also the result of how I had experienced my parents' relationship with one another. In essence, my father had opinions, was the smarter one, and my mother remained mostly passive in her ability to assert her independence. Still, she not only ran a pearl-stringing business but also became an accomplished yoga and swim instructor, for which as I recall she received little joy and acknowledgement from my father

I married an academic who taught and wrote about the Italian resistance movements during World War II. We had three children, Philip, Daniel, and Lydia. Frank was more socialist than Jewish, and after a few years, we moved to Italy with our young children. Frank engaged in research, most notably for a book he wrote about Silvio Trentin, a jurist and partisan with whose family we became lifelong friends. Leftist politics was a strong focus of our life. As Frank's partner, my political sensibilities were nurtured and they grew. We had Maoist friends when they were still chic in Italy, before the Cultural Revolution and Mao's fall from grace. I hated any form of oppression and dictatorship. I was against wars and nuclear proliferation but not against revolutions at the time, although I knew they were bloody. I identified in part as a revolutionary and in another part as a pacifist.

One evening, we were invited to speak at a political meeting of the Italian Communist Party or PCI (Partita Communista Italiana) in Turin, where we lives. Frank had an agenda to speak out against the American war in Vietnam. We sat at a long table on a stage looking out on about 150 party members. They were hostile because we were Americans. I was nervous because I hardly spoke Italian and was once again comforted by the fact that Frank would do the speaking. After two hours of interactions, interruptions, shouting matches, and questions, my husband amazingly won them over. People in the audience clapped, came over to embrace us, and shook our hands. It was a wonderful feeling of connection and quite unexpected, for at the onset the room was filled with hostility.

I played the good wife in the months to come, but eventually I tried to break free, to express myself more independently. I dressed outrageously in long Indian dresses or long skirts with sexy tops that displayed more skin than fabric. I wore oversized earrings as ornate combs held my unruly, waist-length hair carelessly piled on my head. I was tired of being an extension of my worldly, brilliant, and much-sought-after husband. I did not want to be "the professor's wife." My identity transformed to that of a "hippie," and I did not care what anyone thought. The fact that we lived in Turin, a conservative, up-tight, and highly bourgeois city, did not make it easy. I made up for my inability to converse with the intellectuals by refusing to conform to conservative norms. I ached to break loose from anything repressive. I wanted to be free from expectations of who I should be or how I should behave. These expectations never came from Frank directly but rather from the circle of intellectual, high-born Italians we hung out with. The rest of my struggle was internal. I did not know then who I was. Only thirty-one years old, I had a craving for freedom—whatever that meant. Politically, this initial rebellion took me no farther than, "Fuck the system. I don't believe in the Vietnam War, and I don't trust our government." For a refugee who at the time loved America, this was a bold statement within a tepid expression of anarchy.

In 1967, we moved to Cleveland, where Frank was a tenured assistant professor at Case Western Reserve University. It was during the height of the Vietnam War, and we became embroiled in the antiwar movement on campus. Our political life consisted of teach-ins, local demonstrations, marches to Washington, draft counseling, political debates, and fundraisers. In the 1960s, dialogue among us expressed many points of view, for issues were discussed openly and passionately. In our present political climate, this has changed most dramatically. September 11 and the Patriot Act have created an environment of fear and militarism. Back in the Sixties, we strove to make sure the government heard our voices. Our marches in Washington were effective because they were highly organized and allowed diverse antiwar movements to come together with a sense of shared purpose, hope, empowerment, and vitality.

Slowly, I began to speak out. Why was this war continuing? What was our government not telling us? Why the hell were we in Vietnam in the first place?

Indeed, "People Power" was a popular slogan of the time. In addition, dissent was reported in newspapers and on television. Photos of the brutality of war were not yet censored, so the war was visible to Americans. This too had an impact and caused people to question our involvement even further and to rise up in disgust.

Then, there were leaders who guided us and brought us together. Sidney Peck, a sociologist at the university, was especially talented in bringing people together and spearheaded the antiwar movement. He was a tower of strength and infused us with "people power." The country had many progressive antiwar leaders during this historic time. We had Ben Spock as part of our community to further vitalize the strong voices of opposition. I remember dinner parties at his house where he hosted the organizers of the campus movement. All of them were our friends. I will always miss the comradery of that period. One wonderful Saturday in early October 1967, socialist and pacifist minister Norman Thomas, then already in his eighties, was invited to speak on the campus. In our large gymnasium, Frank introduced the tall, formidable figure to a huge, standing-room only crowd of students and professors. We in the campus movement were once again energized and felt a strong solidarity in our friendships and our mutual struggles for a better America. It was a splendid time, and I have rarely since felt so much a part of a common cause that infused us all with love and tremendous hope.

The Sixties and early Seventies were an era of hope for change. We wanted America to be an open society committed to nonviolent and diplomatic solutions. Young and idealistic, we were consumed with the possibility that we could make a difference. Then Kent State happened on the weekend of May 4, 1970, and our right to protest was brutally stopped in its tracks. Student protestors had planned a weekend of nonviolent vigils, teach-ins, and partying at local bars. It was a beautiful campus statement by committed young people. The campus was mobbed when the National Guard was called in by the governor. The guards wore gas masks and high boots. They held tear gas canisters and machine guns ready to fire. The tragedy of it still looms close as I revisit that day. Although I was not there personally, friends who witnessed the event reported the police brutality in detail. The students were in a frenzy after the Guard arrived and the tenor of protest, which had been peaceful, changed. All innocence was lost. The guardsmen were a wild bunch. Four students were murdered: Allison Krause, Sandy Scheuer, William Schroeder, and Jeffrey Miller. They were never closer than 350 feet to their assassins. Nine others were seriously wounded. They remain our children, lost but not forgotten. The violence of the National Guard at Kent State left a permanent mark on the fabric of America. One could no longer feel safe to stand up for what one believed, to resist through gatherings and protests without the threat of violent police action.

During the Sixties, the youth were deeply affected by the drug culture. In my view, it destroyed the drive and energy of the hippie movement for a freer society. I observed how drugs ravished the body and controlled the mind. There would not again be such a focused movement for peace and social change. Together with the Civil Rights movement of the Sixties, the antiwar movement encompassed political, racial, and cultural spheres and exposed a deep schism within 1960s American society. Mark Barringer describes in his essay "The Anti-War Movement in the United States" (from *Encyclopedia of the Vietnam War*, ABC-CLIO):

> The antiwar movement became both more powerful and, at the same time, less cohesive between 1969 and 1973. Most Americans pragmatically opposed escalating the U.S. role in Vietnam, believing the economic cost too high; in November of 1969, a second march on Washington drew an estimated 500,000 participants. At the same time, most disapproved of the counterculture that had arisen alongside the antiwar movement. The clean-cut, well-dressed SDS members, who had tied their hopes to McCarthy in 1968, were being subordinated as movement leaders. Their replacements deservedly gained less public respect, were tagged with the label "hippie," and faced much mainstream opposition from middle-class Americans uncomfortable with the youth culture of the period—long hair, casual drug use, and promiscuity. Protest music, typified by Joan Baez and Bob Dylan, contributed to the gulf between young and old. Cultural and political protest had become inextricably intertwined within the movement's vanguard. The new leaders became increasingly strident, greeting returning soldiers with jeers and taunts, spitting on troops in airports and on public streets.

A unique situation arose in which most Americans supported the cause but opposed the leaders, methods, and culture of protest. The leaders were gone; the young people turned to psychedelics and looked for highs by experimenting with LSD and other hallucinogens. The steam had gone out of the movement; the war had ended and many anarchists of the movement drifted to drugs, became outsiders, or went underground. It is as if hope died. Haight-Ashbury became ground zero for the counterculture.

My son Philip, born on the cusp of the Sixties, would lose his life to the drug culture.

THREE
Liberation

When the women's movement emerged as a radical revolution in the early Seventies, we had moved from Cleveland into our Greenwich Village apartment on Washington Square. Frank was by now a tenured associate professor at Queens College–CUNY. I matriculated toward a Bachelor of Arts degree at Hunter College. The protests and chaos intensified by the ongoing Vietnam War mirrored a rift in our marriage. I was swept up by a new awareness that women could be "liberated" from the tyranny of limited roles. I also found an anchor in women's voices that, to my surprise, echoed my own dissatisfaction. My marriage was in trouble and I had no career. I had given up nursing and was completely unaware there were other women as "stuck" and unfulfilled as I was.

The beginning of my "awakening" occurred one afternoon as I read *The Second Sex* by Simone de Beauvoir in the living room of my apartment. How amazing, I thought, that my life as a wife and mother parallels the lives of other women. What a surprise, for I had felt isolated in my unhappiness. One afternoon, my neighbor and friend Alix Shulman invited me to join her for a Redstocking consciousness-raising meeting. I remember the first meeting, held in a Greenwich Village apartment. I met Ellen Willis, founder of the Redstockings, who would become a powerful voice in progressive feminist politics. Seven women, strangers, sat in a circle as I listened to their words pour out, their frustrations, unfulfilled marriages, and feelings of inferiority to men in a male-dominated society. Exhilarated, I identified with it all.

Once a week, we met in the sanctuary of our safe space. We became sisters and friends—not competitors in the way we had been programmed to relate to other women. I was drawn to the movement like a magnet and became united with women in our struggle for equal rights and freedom. It was a significant time, a true revolution heralding the emergence of woman with a voice of her own and a body that was hers to learn about and to love. We (and I) had felt so repressed, second-class citizens in a world where men had the power. A patriarchal society did not encourage equal rights. Ashamed of our genitals and bodies, we had been sexually passive and unfulfilled. What a revelation! We identified as sex objects, extensions of our husbands. I read once, "a liberated woman was someone who had sex before marriage and a job after" (Gloria Steinem, *New York Magazine* April 4, 1969). Previously, I had never truly formed friendships with women, for they were competitors. That I learned to trust women and form deep, lasting friendships is one of the gifts of the movement that has lasted throughout my life.

Through the early consciousness-raising experience, groups of women spoke to one another about their lives, and our individual voices were beginning to be heard. We were infused with power and creativity, a collective experience that for me meant I was not alone. The movement took us to graduate schools and boardrooms, into science, law, and medicine. We identified that as children, many of our voices had been silenced and relegated to the "second sex." Sisterhood provided us with power and a newly found self-esteem. My sisters would become authors, political writers, and activists. I received my BA degree with a major in philosophy at Hunter College in 1975, when I was forty years old. I had attended part-time in the evening and graduated *cum laude*—quite an accomplishment for someone who graduated high school with grades that barely passed. I would continue on to receive a graduate degree in social work in 1977. During that time, I had decided to enter psychoanalytic training, for I needed to heal myself in the process of working with others to heal themselves.

I am forever indebted to the women who forged ahead to build a powerful political and sexual movement of liberation. My contemporaries were Phyllis Chesler, Shulamith Firestone, Betty Friedan, Gloria Steinem, Germaine Greer, Alix Shulman, Robin Morgan, Ellen Willis, Barbara Seaman, Kate Millet, Susan Sontag, Judith Melina, and the Living Theater. Back then, we wore jump suits bought from a Sears Roebuck catalogue, wore our hair long, used no makeup, and did not shave our legs. Braless, we held our heads high, felt sexy and smart, and supported each other. We spoke up for women's rights and worked for reproductive rights. (To think in 2015, Republican members of Congress still pursue an active agenda to reverse *Roe v. Wade* and deny women's rights to control their own bodies. It remains an endless struggle for freedom of choice.)

We in the movement had marched for abortion rights and later to overturn the Hyde Amendment passed to ban federal spending, including Medicaid, for abortions—as usual on the backs of the poor. In addition, we were sisters struggling together as we began to recognize our own power. This marvelously uplifting moment in a time past provided me with the motivation to look inside myself, to search for who I was. I feel proud that our generation of women provided a legacy for women in future generations. Those years, enhanced by the women's liberation revolution, represented for me a completely divergent path toward freedom of expression and a movement away from the emotional restrictions of my formative years.

I attended a debate held at New York's Town Hall in 1971. Germaine Greer, a strong and outspoken feminist and academic, challenged a young Norman Mailer, whom we all despised at the time because of his condescending attitudes toward women. It was high political theater, and Mailer embodied the essence of the male chauvinist who patronized and denigrated women and who feminists vowed to confront and resist. I could only recognize Mailer's literary genius and political dynamism for progressive causes decades after I had shed my revolutionary fervor. For my son Dan, who also has literary capabilities, Mailer was an icon and role model, a strong assertive man. In earlier years, I had accused Mailer of being a misogynist. Dan and I battled out our divergent points of view for several years.

Consciousness-raising groups in the early Seventies became an effective way for women to explore topics such as family life, education, sex, and work from their personal perspectives. As we shared our stories, we began to understand ourselves in relation to the patriarchal society we lived in, and this is how we discovered our commonalities and could then build solidarity. I began to see myself as part of a larger population of women.

Collectively with other women's voices, I slowly trusted myself to speak out, to express a cause I believed in: equal rights for women in the workplace and in bed; we discovered we had a right to feel our sexuality and to love ourselves as women. How fantastic to discuss orgasms and to discover how many women never experienced one. We discussed differences between clitoral and vaginal orgasms, as if all taboos and myths about women's bodies could finally be lifted. We learned to give ourselves orgasms through masturbation as we explored our bodies without shame. It was as if a dammed-up river suddenly had burst free as we explored and wrote about the role of women in our society, the politics of women, the rejection of women as second-class citizens who were merely sex objects. I longed to let go of how I looked or how to please my husband, this self-consciousness that bypassed who I really was and what I thought about. I no longer wanted to be an extension of my husband. Best of all, I discovered I was not alone in my unhappy, frustrated marriage, for my sisters had also faked orgasms and felt stifled and not heard. We sat together weekly, eight or ten of us in someone's living room. The Redstockings brought me to a new self-awareness and raised many questions about how I wanted to live my life. During this important period of time, I was in graduate school with three children and a troubled marriage.

It was in the mid-Seventies, the decade my marriage ended, that I completed graduate school with a degree in social work. Unhappiness, fueled by the emotional roller coaster of my marriage, propelled me to seek out the first of many therapists. I had such difficulty expressing myself yet my sensitivity and creative spirit needed to be unleashed. I had not yet found a direction and suffered from depression and anxiety, as well as feeling completely stuck. During my years with Frank, I had discovered a political side of me that resonated with freedom from all forms of human rights

Lillian's children Dan and Lydia, 1991.

abuses, oppression, repression, and racism. I had written poetry from the time I was eighteen. In my early twenties, I was violently opposed to McCarthyism and wrote about it. Frank, my academic husband, wrote about the Resistance and struggles against Fascism in Italy. I was attracted to the cause but had no idea how to channel my interests.

Despite our problems, during eighteen years together there had been excitement, a seductive intensity with Frank that drew me in just when I thought I could no longer love him. My suffering heightened when Frank drank or expressed anger. There was never physical danger, but I perceived my life as unstable. My labile moods were dependent on alternating calm or chaos in my relationship with Frank. Externally driven to some degree, but more importantly, I came to recognize this as the state of my internal self. I had three children and no monetary resources. I was afraid and believed I was

Dan and Lydia, 2015.

unable to live without Frank, so dependent was I on him. Fear had transformed me into a victim. In our home, one never knew what to expect. I would have wanted to be a steady parent, to provide a sense of familiarity for our children. It was impossible. My antennae were on guard and I attempted to control a situation by anticipating the emotional climate of the moment. I am not saying our troubled family life was the cause of Phil's addiction a few years later, but it was surely a contributing factor.

Frank and I often spent our summers apart. When he was away in Italy, involved in research for another book, the calm interludes refreshed me. Our passionate letters to one another reflected our desire to have a happier life. It was easier to feel love from a distance. During the summer of 1972, three years before we were to separate, I took Phil, Dan, and Lydia, then thirteen, eleven, and nine, to Bonnieux in the south of France. Phil and Dan were close then. They loved to sing, "He ain't heavy, he's my brother," as Phil carried Dan on his back. They would giggle and finish off with an arm wrestle. Phil would let Dan win. Saying good-bye to their daddy, Phil helped me to negotiate our bags and was supportive during our long wait in Marseille. There had been a strike that kept us at the airport for fourteen hours. All three were genuinely excited about our adventure. Phil, so full of energy, life, and promise, had not yet become acquainted with the demons of his doom. I was ambivalent about a two-month separation from Frank with three children alone in a foreign country, yet I had a strong need to get away. I chose Bonnieux because my friend Jef Majors and her lover Andre lived there as expatriates. She had encouraged me to come. The former wife of a Case Western physics professor, Jef, and her former husband John, had been our friends in Cleveland. She found us a tiny house in the center of the village, next door to a bakery and antique store. The house resembled an above-ground cave: dark, with two tiny bedrooms, and in the back, an overgrown jungle masquerading as a garden. We settled into our little French hideaway, and I wrote every day to Frank. I tried to adjust to two months in this strange little village where I spoke miserable French and couldn't quite relish the beautiful countryside.

Time passed slowly as church bells chimed every half hour. Sometimes I wondered what I was doing there and why I had come. Yet, it was a relief to be away. My troubled marriage seemed to be solid again from afar, my dreams of our love rekindled from a distance. Bonnieux was a special time when my three children and I were close and together. I still had the illusion that Frank and I could make it together. Despite my newfound assertiveness and increased self-confidence gained from the women's movement, it remained difficult for me to let go of aspects of my marriage that gave me monetary comfort and a reasonable degree of comradery with Frank. Alcoholism and our emotional incompatibility drove us to a final split in 1977 and divorce in 1978. It was a difficult time and the start of a new chapter of my life.

FOUR

Lilli and Fritz

It was six in the morning that summer in 1983. The walls of my bedroom closed around me. I could not breathe and coughed violently as if to expunge myself from last night's conversation with my father. His tired voice sounded overwhelmed and weary. "Hi, Lillian. Your mother has left the house again. She walked out in her nightgown and is worse than ever. She told me she hates me but then, I am used to that." He still had his familiar German accent but spoke fluent English. What did he want me to do? As if he had read my mind, he said, "It's much worse, but I know she will come home again soon." Relieved not to have to drive to Bayside, I told him to call me if he needed me to come out.

In the previous two years, my mother had started to act in a newly bizarre manner. She sang incessantly with words designed to attack my father. Her favorite song to him, "Rind fie" (not a literal translation, but meant as "dirty pig"), made her laugh. She put down my father in many ways and at times depicted him as a garbage can. She was ornery, angry, manic, and high as a kite. Sometimes she ran out of the house only to return some hours later. No one knew where she had been. After some weeks, she invariably sank into silence and barely spoke. My mother's mood changes became increasingly dramatic. When high, she talked nonstop and wore bizarre clothing. Her favorite activity was to attach numerous bathing caps to herself with safety pins, perhaps ten or twelve. One day, she put on a bathing suit under her dress and danced around as she rid herself of the dress. My mother, a certified Red Cross swim instructor, now parodied her proud accomplishment with a clownish persona. She spoke in numerous, completely unfamiliar tongues that we had never heard before. Her venom and repressed anger simply burst through without censorship. Other times she might display a charming, girlish, and spontaneous innocence. Had it taken her sixty-eight years to express herself? Now, she could finally be herself within the bizarre episodes of her manic craziness. My father and sister liked to pretend nothing was wrong when they were with her, but my father grew exhausted and often short-tempered. Their moods changed together. With my father, there could be no honest response. When manic, my mother became enraged toward my father. My father, in turn, replied with an overbearing niceness in response to her humiliating words. "You are my wonderful Lilli," he would say, a continuous dance of pretend. That drove me crazy to the point that I preferred to stay away. Fritz infantilized my mother by over-accommodating her behavior. Eventually he would turn to anger. The way I remember it, my sister, Carol, was in a terrible position as she simultaneously tried to soothe Lilli while supporting all of our father's actions. My sister, in the middle, tried to please both parents. This surely was a terrible burden, as she lived with them.

"I don't know how long I can keep this up," my father said.

One day, he had enough. "Lilli, I am taking you to a psychiatrist," he announced to my mother. She did not resist that first time. The psychiatrist met my parents, sister, and me in the psychiatric emergency room of Long Island Jewish Hospital. My mother had attached several bathing caps to her dress and stretched two caps over her head. She sang and swayed her hips, exuberant as an unleashed puppy. As she approached the doctor she clapped her hands and danced.

"*Bonjour, mon cheri!*" she called out cheerfully. Then she continued to speak the unknown language.

"Lilli, do you know where you are?" queried the doctor. He was a tall, unattractive man who spoke in a matter-of-fact, emotionally dead manner. My mother, oblivious, oozed her charm and flirted outrageously. She stood close to him and with a wide, toothy smile answered, "Well of course, *mon cheri*, I am in the hospital. Where do you think we are?" Seductive as I had never seen her, she danced around in flagrant chaos and moved her arms about wildly. Her life, the spontaneity snuffed out by strict German parents, had been repressed and controlled to produce an anxious, harsh, and unhappy woman. She was exhilarated now. How sad to see her like this, here in a hospital for the crazy ones. My mother danced over to me and said loud enough for everyone to hear, "Gisela, I don't like this doctor. He looks like a devil." My father and sister were embarrassed, but I agreed with her. I put my arm around her and whispered in her ear, "It's all right, my little Mommy."

This was the first and only time my mother would allow herself to be hospitalized voluntarily. There had been an opportunity here to help her. The doctors could not figure out how to characterize her illness. She was an enigma. "Schizophrenia" is what they finally came up with. Bipolar illness, then called manic depression, was not even considered because the staff was unfamiliar with such a late onset. Yet, she was blatantly manic. I knew my mother was not schizophrenic in the same way I knew my son's onset of "schizophrenia" some years later had been directly related to twenty hits of LSD in his freshman year of college. With both, the bipolar component had been left untreated. My mother was admitted and given large doses of Thorazine, one of the early neuroleptics for psychosis. Somehow the dose knocked her out so that she could barely move. She became jaundiced and lifeless. All her life, my mother had been sensitive to drugs and had chosen not to take them. Philip, some years later, would have horrendous side effects from Thorazine. My mother had always preferred natural healing. I knew she had received too high a dose to be therapeutic, and I tried to express my views to the resident on her unit without response. After a few days, my mother became sicker. She had signed herself into the hospital voluntarily to receive help. Instead, she was misdiagnosed and overmedicated. Ultimately, she had enough; she refused further treatment and my father took her home.

For some years, my mother went in and out of her illness. Her mania was interspersed with bouts of depression. It was during those times I felt closest to her. I would go up to her room where she lay on the bed. "Come here, Gisela; sit next to me," she would say. Then she reached out her arms to pull me close to her. I felt most loved during her depressed cycles when she was vulnerable and emotional. She was able to cry then as my head rested on her, so close I could feel her heart beat.

My father took care of her, and during that time, on the advice of a psychiatrist and against my mother's will, he spiked her tea with Haldol, another neuroleptic to contain her and keep her passive. It infuriated me how my father and sister could agree to this deception as a way to control my mother. I watched my mother become at times a meek, voiceless child, not in control of her own life, an echo of how I had felt growing up. My father's controlling behavior and my sister's complicit acceptance left me enraged. I could feel little empathy for him and what he was going through

Still, at other times, she continued her virulent attacks on my father. She wanted no part of him when she was manic. Everyone felt sorry for my father. I could not tolerate to hear his alternately controlling and then patronizing behavior. His words to her were hollow. "Look at Lilli; she is the best wife," he would say as he tried to be patient as I nearly choked. "Dad, she will never take responsibility for her illness. You are treating her like a child and you are giving her no choices," I would plead with him, to no avail. He remained overwhelmed, angry, and tremendously unhappy. Carol, as always, supported my father's actions. He was master, and what he did was right; there was no other way.

The whole mess was awful. I felt useless, stayed away, and put the responsibility on my sister, who was trapped with them. At times my father was hateful and tormented my mother. "You are a stupid asshole," he would say to her, or "I should have married Ursula. How did I end up with you?" There were other times when they clung together and spoke of their love for one another. Carol, the mediator, most likely kept them from killing each other. Throughout the years, although she had unsuccessfully attempted to leave home and make a life for herself elsewhere, Carol did not have the emotional capacity, the strength to stay away, to make her own life. Looking back, I realize I might have helped her to separate by offering support and love. Instead, I can barely remember the times she tried to leave but recognize, with regret, the disconnect between us.

One day, my mother sold toilet paper in front of a local church two blocks from their house. "Toilet paper to wipe your behind! Only ten cents!" she sang as loud as she could. Then, as if that wasn't bad enough, she wrapped herself around a lamppost and sang "Lili Marlene" for hours. The priest called the police who took her to Jamaica Hospital psychiatric emergency room. My father had become ill with flu-like symptoms. I had been in close contact with Jamaica Hospital, and after a week, a psychiatrist called me. "What do you want us to do with her? We'll take her anywhere her husband designates," he said over the phone. "We have not heard from him. Do you know where he is? Can you reach him? We need to hear from him or we will transfer her to the state hospital, Creedmoor." I didn't know what was going on. Why had no one heard from my father? I wanted my mother to be transferred to a private hospital. I called my father. "Dad, the hospital needs to transfer Mom. They want to know what to do with her. If no one intervenes, she will be sent to Creedmoor. Dad, that's a state hospital; please don't let them send her there." After a few moments, I heard my father's voice, slow and deliberate. "Let them take her to Creedmoor. I can't take it anymore. I have had it. I'm finished." He hung up.

I was in a troubled place, full of fear. My mother went to Creedmoor and fortunately responded well to lithium, used successfully for bipolar illness. My father, in the meantime, had been admitted to Long Island Jewish Hospital. At first, his internist dismissed the flu-like symptoms, and he was told to rest at home. Three weeks later, my father developed osteomyelitis in his spine. My parents had used this internist for their yearly checkups. They felt they were in good hands. Yet, how did my father's flu become so serious? I did not think he had been treated properly at the onset of his symptoms, but my father would not hear of it. He believed in his doctor. When I visited him at Long Island Jewish Hospital, he had been given strong doses of antibiotics intravenously. My father, who had never been sick before, looked vulnerable, older than I had ever seen him.

Lilli and Fritz.

"Gisela, I am in such pain. I saw an orthopedic surgeon yesterday. He told me that if I do not have my spine fused, I will not be able to walk again. I am going to have it done." I was horrified and deeply concerned. "But why so fast, Dad? Aren't you having a second opinion? That's very drastic. It's important to make sure and not take the first opinion." My father, who rarely questioned authority responded, "I have made up my mind. I like this surgeon and I am going to follow his treatment." He had not spoken of my mother since her breakdown. Neither of them had mentioned the other. My parents, together for fifty-three years, were both ill in separate hospitals.

That night I dreamed I was on a bus. Across the aisle sat a very old, deeply wrinkled woman, her walker next to her—an old child dependent on her stone-faced nanny. What had her life been like? Did she have family once? The old woman-child fumbled to open her worn, nearly empty pocketbook as her caregiver stared straight ahead. I was touched by the pain of dying without love, in the hands of a stranger.

I was shocked to see my father following twelve hours of surgery, when steel rods were inserted into his back and fused. He would require a second follow-up surgery. He lay on his pillow and at age seventy- nine had become a shrunken old man in a deep depression. He put his hand in mine and said, "Gisela, you were right. I should have listened to you." To see my father like this was almost unbearable, but to have become aware of his "mistake" was tragic. My sister tended to both our parents every day as she moved from one hospital to the next. That day, after my father's surgery, I walked outside and could do no more than sit on the side of a curb and weep. I remember it all so well, alone in a situation that felt intolerable. I was completely estranged from my parents, who were lost to one another. Divorced myself, for a few moments I did not know how to go on. This moment of despair passed as quickly as it came over me.

When I returned the next day, a doctor pulled me aside outside my father's room. He said, "Your father is terribly depressed, and he tells me that he wants to die. We are thinking of moving him onto a psychiatric unit." I heard myself speak. "If you dare to move my father into a psychiatric unit, I will sue you and the hospital. This is a man who rescued me, my mother, and many relatives from Nazi Germany. Do you hear me?" I could not tolerate both my parents on a psychiatric unit, and so I reacted rather than discussed a viable action to help my father move out of his depression. My father remained in his room for another ten days and then was temporarily discharged to be readmitted in three weeks for more surgery. Carol took on the responsibility for his care. I was angry again with my father and recoiled at the rigidity of his fixed position. That he had been unable to consider alternatives, I believe, contributed to his physical deterioration and ultimate death. The German rigidity, something I had always been so aware of, a trait I did not wish for myself, affected me strongly, and so I was relieved to stay away. So much had been left unsaid between us, and I, fraught with ambivalence, guilt, and longing, still yearned for the father who had so bitterly disappointed me.

My father remained despondent. Surely it was temporary. How could both my parents be in a major depression at the same time? Neither could ever acknowledge their own darkness to the other. Their fears had remained unexamined until they imploded into the nightmare each now lived separately. I could not tolerate being caught in the belly of psychosis and hospitals again. I wanted none of it, so I stayed away.

It was May 16, 1986, and I was about to complete my Individual Psychoanalytic and Group Therapy trainings. In the therapists' lounge at the Postgraduate Center in New York, I waited for the time to lead my group. Someone called out, "Phone for you, Lillian." I picked up the receiver to hear Carol's voice. "Lillian." There was a long silence. Then, "Papi is dead. He killed himself."

What was I doing here at the center leading my own life while my sister was witness to a suicide? "I'm coming," I said. "I'll be there as soon as I can."

My father had managed to walk down the cellar steps to hang himself while my sister was out buying groceries. "It's not your fault; it's not your fault, Carol," I told her repeatedly. Two days before, I had dismissed Dan's call after a visit to see his grandfather. "Mom, Opa asked me to get him a gun. He wants to die." I blew it off and am still haunted by my carelessness. It was almost as if my unspoken message to my father had been, "You deserve to die because you were not able to question authority." I had contempt for the passivity he stood for. Yet I too remained passive and could not let myself question more effectively my father's decisions.

In Bayside, I went down to the basement where my father lay, his face soft and completely relaxed. He looked the way I remembered him—not in pain, a younger Fritz, my German dad, my heritage. He had freed himself from his burdens. I sat down on the cellar floor next to him and wept. I wish I had seen him one more time. I wish I had said goodbye. I recall his words, spoken to me so often over the years, "If I should ever be so ill that I should become a burden, my wish is that I will be able to do myself in." And so he did.

Carol.

Could I have stopped his suicide? I obsessed about this question. But how could I have? By restraining him? Should I have let my father be treated for depression in the hospital and be transferred to the psychiatric floor? Why had I been so uninvolved? Could I ever make it up to my sister? A family in chaos is what was left of the hope for a better life.

My mother was still in Creedmoor. Since the day she was picked up by the police in front of the church so many months before, she had not seen my father. After Carol and I arrived on her unit to tell her of our father's illness and subsequent suicide, we sat down and took hold of her hands. She was so small and vulnerable on this God-awful unit at Creedmoor. My mother sat quietly for a moment and said, "Fritz has died, hasn't he?" She cried as we held her in our arms. She knew. "Fritz would have been worried about me, and he would not have stayed away," she said.

We had a simple graveside ceremony at Wellwood Cemetery. Those present included Carol, Dan, a handful of friends, and Frank, who loved my father. I do not understand why I encouraged Lydia to stay away from my father's graveside service. She had been taking her final exams, an undergraduate then at the University of Wisconsin. Was I trying to shield her? I am reminded of the funeral of my grandmother that I had not been allowed to attend. I wish I had encouraged Lydia to come home. I can honestly not recall whether Phil was there or not. This disturbs me. It was three years after an eight-month hospitalization period at New York hospital, Westchester division. It had been a period of time when Phil had remained clean and some healing occurred. Yet some memories are muddled and others have found a place of rest. I do know he loved my father.

My mother, accompanied by an aide, looked elegant and carried herself with dignity. She wore a dress my grandmother had crocheted for her so many years ago and a small diamond necklace my father had given her for their twenty-fifth anniversary. How proud I was of her that day. Her face was solemn, composed, and utterly beautiful. She was discharged from Creedmoor one week later and lived with Carol four more years, well-stabilized on lithium. That my mother was able to stay with me at my Riverside Drive apartment for a few weeks was wonderful for us. It was the first time we had been alone together, and it was a precious and healing time.

Several months later, Lilli died of a massive stroke. I had spoken with her on the phone about an hour before and had promised to come to Bayside that weekend for a visit.

FIVE
Philip

During the summer of 1988, I received a call from Philip. "Mom, I'm converting to Catholicism. The service is on September 9, High Mass at 8 p.m. I want you to come. It's going to be at Saint Anthony's Church. I've been studying with Father Pat Doyle. A wonderful man, Mom. I want you to meet him."

Phil had often attended Mass at St. Anthony's, a church he loved, adjacent to his Greenwich Village studio apartment on Sullivan Street in Soho. Phil was five foot eleven and slender, his face expressive and sensitive. He was clean-shaven, although on occasion he might grow a full beard that complimented his handsome face. I loved his beautiful brown eyes and the way his mouth curled up into a smile whenever he greeted me. I never considered he would convert to Catholicism. It must give him something, I thought. He was excited and happy. I was conscious of how keenly my antennae were assessing the sound of his voice despite eight years of sobriety. I had always been able to tell when he was high. "I'm great, Mom. Put the date on your calendar. Catholicism brings me closer to God. Have to go now. Talk to you soon. Love you." In a moment, he was gone.

I thought again about Phil's complaints of no spiritual life in our home. He was right, of course. Frank and I had turned our backs on our Jewish heritage and substituted politics. Could it be this "lack" within our family life that had contributed to Phil's drug addiction? How easy it was to blame myself, Frank, our politics, our marital problems... Perhaps it was an affliction of guilt designated for parents with troubled children. Yet, what roots did I have? I had run away from my refugee experience, my German and mostly my Jewish roots. Now none of this mattered. Only Phil's well-being was important. So there I was on September 9, attending High Mass at St. Anthony's Church. I found Lisa, his longtime girlfriend, greeted her with a hug, and sat next to her in the pew. No other family members were present. Dan and Lydia thought Phil's obsession with religion for most of his adult life was one more sign of his instability. His father was not present. I knew Phil was healing after his long journey with drugs and mental illness, brought on by too many hits of LSD while in his freshman year of college that would trigger his fall into psychosis. I had to be grateful for his eight years of sobriety.

At the church, I let myself sink into the mood and watched the handsome young priest, Father Doyle, walk down the aisle. Four young men and one woman dressed in white robes trailed behind him. They held candles as they walked slowly toward the altar. The darkened church reflected silhouettes of candlelight, housed in ornate candelabra along both sides of the aisle. Father Doyle carried two incense burners, one in each hand. He waved his arms up, down, and around. A moment of peace enveloped me inside the insular cocoon of the church, Phil's church. My son's face shone with pride. Our eyes met, our faces soft. At that moment Phil looked so much like my father, and I remembered Phil was the son of a German Jewish mother who had fled Nazi Germany with her parents. I knew that would never change regardless of the external circumstances. What did it matter how Phil found solace? What did it matter, the degree of religion practiced or not practiced by Phil or by the Jews of Nazi Germany? Those who could not escape were slaughtered.

I turned fifty-four in March 1989. Phil was clean as far as I knew. I longed to nurture a spiritual part of me not cultivated through organized religion. I was exhausted and depressed from the ups and downs of Phil's addiction. My father's suicide and mother's death had taken over so much of my life and energy. Lydia and Dan suffered. (Their stories are left out of this book.) It is still difficult for me to divest completely from pangs of guilt; I would have liked to have been so much more of a parent for them.

I decided to take a "healing" trip and joined a group of hikers to trek in the Himalayas of Northern India. An interest in Buddhism emerged as I wandered the high passes. In Leh, capital of Ladakh, I felt exhilarated perched on a mountain 12,000 feet above sea level.

The surrounding moonscape was surreal, devoid of greenery due to the high altitude. Rainbows across the mountains created a stark beauty such as I had never seen. High snow-jeweled mountain passes, combined with air so thin and light, spoke of other-worldliness as each breath filled me with possibility, clarity, and hope. I walked across the rocks, the magnificent terrain along the edge of the mountain, and was overcome with emotion. Everything I thought I knew or did not understand was transformed into clarity. Clouds so close that I could touch them, this other world sat 3,000 feet above the tree line. I stood on this unknown earth where shadows chased sunlight across mountain peaks as I breathed in the purity of the air that cleansed me. On this stark, rocky, otherworldly, mysterious place with a group of six others and our guides, we moved slowly to the highest pass. I would eventually reach a 16,000-foot pass named Matho La. How spectacular! I felt proud of my accomplishment.

We camped for the night at 15,000 feet, and despite my headache, Diamox kept altitude sickness at a minimum. Our tents had been placed next to a Matho family, eight children, sheep, and goats. They were migratory and lived during the summer months in stone dwellings. Ten people slept together on a dirt kitchen floor. How charming they were, gracious and kind as we spoke with our eyes and our hearts. Barriers and differences melted away for we had met each other with interest, curiosity, and delight. I think of them still. I have always felt this open, interested curiosity when I am fortunate enough to be in a new and different culture. I would also feel this way upon my first visits to Israel/Palestine, where I met both Israelis and Palestinians.

I felt an inexplicable spiritual connection to Ladakh and the surrounding monasteries. Within the stark beauty, it was Buddha, not god but a mortal man, who helped to clarify my search for man's connection to others and the unity of wisdom and compassion. It was here I encountered for the first time hundreds of wind horses. Red, green, white, blue, and yellow little prayer flags flew across the landscape. They were everywhere. The mythical wind horse inhabits every single prayer flag. This Tibetan creature is said to combine the speed of wind and strength of a horse. In Tibetan mythology, wind horses are called upon in the face of suffering by all beings in search of transformation and good fortune. I imagined myself on the back of the wind horse, in search of transformation and a spiritual contact with my own dead ancestors. This was accomplished through meditation, where I learned to discover the spirit of oneness with the universe. I continue to love the little flags, caressed by wind as they dance mischievously across the sky. To this day they grace the entrance of my log house and fill me with joy.

Phil began to use drugs at age sixteen and never made it through his college freshman year. Instead he took LSD and was transformed. "I'm the Messiah, Mom." He had found Jesus. He also found the "Born-Again Christians," or rather, they found him. Young men dressed in suits and ties came to my apartment to preach fundamentalism. So completely antithetical to my philosophy, my roots as a German Jew, I could hardly feel anything except disgust. Yet I listened to their words and was determined to remain silent and respectful because Phil was enamored with them. The Born-Agains reached out to Phil and drew him in. They offered protection and Jesus to the vulnerable ones.

I had wanted Phil to see a psychiatrist, which he vehemently rejected. The Born-Agains said he could be saved through faith. That resonated for Phil, who walked a fine line between madness and reality, and so he chose to walk with them. For a time, he even found solace. He would go off with them, sometimes for weeks, as they searched for converts. He was looked after, and to my knowledge, he was briefly content. Relieved, I knew he had found a temporary new home. As he walked with them for several weeks to proselytize, Phil's religious obsession with Jesus became the focus of his life and remained with him until his death. He read the New Testament and begged me to read it also, which I did. We read the King James Edition to each other and I saw his face relax. Haunted by a sense of my failure, I embraced Phil's temporary saviors who, for a short time,

Philip.

comforted him. Ultimately, it ceased to matter how he found comfort. When Phil began to wear a cross on a chain around his neck, I knew it was precious to him. That was all that mattered to me.

It had been the mission of the Born-Agains to collect "lost souls" for conversion. Phil did not last long. Apparently too crazy even for them, he returned home and fell into a further downhill decline. His first hospitalization happened in 1981. He was twenty-one.

"I'm ready to go to the hospital, Mom," Phil announced one July morning as we were having tea together. I had been pushing and urging for weeks. "Phil, I'm so glad; let's get ready." I smiled with relief. Now Phil would finally receive help. Soon after, we walked together to the psychiatric emergency room at St. Vincent's Hospital. The place was chaotic. We announced ourselves and then just sat. It seemed like forever as I watched Phil play with the silver cross and chain. He held it in his hand, let it dangle in front of his eyes, and stared into space. I felt nauseous. The nurse finally came and reached out her hand to Phil. "Pray for me, Mom; pray to Jesus," he said as he was led into the evaluation room. A moment later, I was overcome with light-headedness. My heart pounded hard, and I began to sweat profusely. Overcome with nausea, I grabbed the side of a garbage can and began to retch. Was I having a heart attack? Would I die in this awful place? My stomach heaved violently and I needed to sit down on the floor right then. Fatigue took over. I stood up after three deep yoga breaths. How did it come to this? My son completely lost and praying to Jesus? Did he find solace? He was the son of a German Jew, a refugee. Strange I somehow needed to repeat this over again to remember who I was or perhaps who Phil was. I found a phone and called Frank. He was by then remarried. "Phil's in the emergency room at St Vincent's. Can you come?" When I saw Frank arrive, I was grateful not to be alone. Instead, what is etched in my memory is Frank's face enraged that I had not called him sooner, furious that our son was psychotic, furious with me. He could offer me no support.

Our son was admitted to Reiss 6 Psychiatric Unit of St Vincent's Hospital. When I approached the floor that afternoon, the resident rushed toward me and led me straight to his office. Frank was nowhere in sight. I sat across from the doctor and tried to hide my nervousness. I stared at his face. He is so young, I could be his mother, I thought. "Look, your son is very sick," the doctor began. His voice broke through my thoughts. "We think he is paranoid schizophrenic and are starting him on neuroleptics. He thinks everyone is after him and believes that God is speaking to him." I sat for a moment, incredulous, and then responded. "We have no schizophrenia in our family, but there is bipolar disorder on my mother's side, and I think on my father's also. You should know that Phil's obsession with God started when he took acid last year in college. He had at least twenty hits. That's when he started to go crazy." Didn't this doctor know that popping LSD can induce a paranoid schizophrenic reaction? That's what Timothy Leary's research had shown. I had read it all, and more.

I continued, "Phil was always social and related with other people. Drugs changed all that. Listen, please listen to me; my son does not have schizophrenia." I felt my emotions take over. I needed to stay calm.

The preoccupied young resident spoke again. "I was raised in the South, and I have needed to keep far away from fanatic religions. Quite frankly, your son's bizarre obsession with Jesus is frightening." Was I really hearing this from the doctor who was supposed to treat my son? Was he ignorant as well as naïve?

"But you are the doctor. Haven't you seen religious delusions before? They are part of an acute psychotic break." I hoped he would say something to inspire confidence. At least Phil was safe in the hospital, and I hoped there would be other psychiatrists involved. The doctor told me to go home for the rest of the day and return tomorrow.

I left the unit exhausted and found Frank outside the locked door. I saw his sad eyes, and his mouth pressed tight. I threw my arms around him, and for a moment found comfort. I was incredibly sad, and I also knew Phil's illness caused his father great pain. Still I was relieved to think Phil would now receive help.

The next day, I arrived on the unit and was shocked. Overnight, Phil's gait had changed to a part shuffle, his neck and head stretched back. He couldn't straighten his head. They must have pumped him up with medication. My worst fears were realized. I stormed up to the nurses' station. "Hasn't anyone noticed my son has been over-medicated? He shouldn't be walking with his neck extended and his head bent back!" There was no response as I pleaded for them to take a look. I was simply told not to worry. Phil took my hand and pulled me down the hall. What a pitiful sight the two of us must have been. We reached a closet. Phil opened the door and told me, "Jesus was calling me into the closet; he spoke to me from the ceiling." He stared at the ceiling as I stood with him. It was a terrible moment.

Phil's flagrant, bizarre, wild psychosis left as dramatically as it had come. He was better within a week. The drugs were adjusted and the religious preoccupations ceased. Phil decided to sign himself out against all our advice. We knew he wasn't ready, but he felt good, he said, and he wanted no more of the hospital. He was twenty-one and no one could stop him. He stayed on his medication for a few weeks and then refused to take them. There was no follow-up protocol because he had left against advice. That decision led to a cycle of future hospitalizations. With each admission, it took longer for him to come out of the psychosis. He was hospitalized a second time at St. Vincent's and a few months later at Roosevelt Hospital. People tried to help get him into a rehab, to no avail. Phil wanted none of it. They were dark times for he became more and more bizarre. Neither his father nor I knew what to do. He frightened me as he descended into hell.

Phil's moods were volatile, and he was often delusional. On May 16, 1981, he walked into my apartment and announced, "Mom, I went to Tavern on the Green and told the people sitting there I would shoot all the Nazis. The Nazis threw me out." I called his father, and he came by soon after. Phil sat stone-faced on the couch. In an effort to bring levity to this awful moment, I blurted to Frank, "He wants help, thank God." I sat down next to Phil. His face was vacant, lost. It was all so pathetic. I could no longer find my son. It had taken me months of soul-searching to realize that I had no other choice but to have Phil committed involuntarily. Frank had helped me to accept this. It was horrendous to imagine that Phil would now be doomed to psychiatric hospitals and never get out. I had little faith in the treatment of mental illness. I had seen too many failures, but there was no choice now. Phil was willing to go into a cab with Frank. "We will find you help," Frank told Phil gently. For a moment, Phil put his trust into his dad. I had begged Frank to take Phil without me. I could not bring myself to face the prospect of leaving my son at Bellevue. I hated Bellevue. For me to enter those locked doors was to enter the doors of hell and hopelessness. I thought that only the poorest, homeless, criminally ill, and lost souls were admitted to Bellevue. Not my son.

I found out later the trip to Bellevue had been a nightmare. Phil struggled to get out of the cab and bit Frank. It had been a fierce struggle. When he called me later, Frank was completely exhausted. "I left Phil in the emergency room. He will be admitted," he told me. The receiver clicked and I was alone. I was tormented over Phil's loss of freedom, the snake pit misery of Bellevue, the insensitivity of the overburdened staff, the untrained abusive aides and the physical ugliness and squalor. I slept fitfully that first night as demons occupied my dreams. I assumed Phil would be moved from the emergency room to the psychiatric unit within a relatively short time.

The next morning I received a phone call from my neighbor, Lucinda. A registered nurse, she had by chance worked the night shift in the Bellevue psychiatric emergency room the day Phil came to be admitted. She had some startling news. "Lillian, you won't believe who I saw last night. What a surprise when I saw Phil tied to a wheelchair! He spent the night there. I felt so sorry for him." All I could hear was "tied to a wheelchair."

"Please tell me what you know, Lucinda," I pleaded.

"Oh, Lillian," she continued. "He tried to get away and the staff threatened him with a needle in his eye if he did not sit still." My mind played tricks on me. I had a sudden thought that perhaps Phil needed to experience the darkest chaos of his illness without being continually cushioned by his parents. Perhaps only then would he be motivated toward recovery. This was how I managed to cope with the news from my neighbor. What I really thought was, No! This is not a way to treat any human being. This is degrading, an assault on the spirit and human dignity.

Phil must have been heavily medicated at the time. He told me later that he did not remember the experience. It would be three days before I found the courage to visit him. I think I needed to disengage in order to get back my strength. I asked Lydia, who was by then seventeen, whether she would come with me, and she was willing. Dan stayed away. Phil's craziness had always been frightening for him. It was simply too close to his own struggles.

Lydia's presence gave me strength and courage. We arrived at Bellevue and were told Phil was on unit PQ3. As we walked the gray maze of corridors, my heart pounded in tune with the rapid steps we were taking. We entered a huge day room with forbidding barred windows, steel tables, and cheap chairs. Ashen faces milled about. Harsh overhead lights highlighted the barren chill of the surroundings.

We saw Phil, who walked over to us with huge strides. He looked wild yet totally at home, comfortable with his blackened feet in hospital flip-flops, his disheveled clothes and matted hair. He greeted us as if he owned the place. He walked to and fro with an air of confidence as he spoke to other lost ones in this sea of despair. I made brief contact with a mother, as if to make sure this was real and not a scene from one of the circles of hell. Her son had been a child prodigy, a Julliard graduate and concert pianist. She appeared old and worn, her face sad beyond description. Meanwhile, Phil flitted around the God-awful dayroom with surreal vomit-yellow walls. Yet, he smiled his charming smile. I could see he wasn't suffering, but I was. What world is this, I wondered. How did it come to this? Who is he? Who am I? Who is crazy? If there is a God, please help me! Phil's admission to Bellevue was a further descent into chaos, but it was also the beginning of a torturous road toward a ten-year recovery period and a time when Phil remained drug-free. Best of all, Dr. Kirshenbaum, a psychiatrist Phil had eventually agreed to see for a consultation, had come through for us after I had called him with the frantic news. He arranged for Phil to be transferred out of Bellevue, and on June 12, 1982, Phil was taken by ambulance to New York Hospital, where he stayed for six months.

Between 1970 and Phil's admission to "Bloomingdales," as the psychiatric hospital was referred to, I decided I no longer wanted to pursue a career in nursing and no longer wanted to work in a hospital. I had been in therapy since the early Seventies when my marriage began to crumble, and my therapist's interest in me provided the impetus to enter a Master's degree program in social work. I had a goal to practice psychoanalysis. I am convinced the pressures of school helped me survive emotionally and eased the chaos of my life. After graduate school, I worked in child welfare and part-time in a mental health clinic. Accepted at an analytic training institute in

1981, I began psychoanalytic training combined with three days a week of personal psychoanalysis. Despite my divorce, Phil's deterioration and breakdown, and the problems of parenting Dan and Lydia as teenagers, I was able to train in a profession where I ultimately hoped to heal myself.

Phil remained psychotic for five months. The social worker talked of a possible transfer to Manhattan State Hospital because they did not know whether Phil would come out of his psychosis. I could not have heard anything more frightening. I had to find a way to let him stay longer. Instinctively, I felt he would get better, but it would take more time. They gave him four more weeks. Then, quite spontaneously, Phil moved out of his psychosis and plunged into that dark depression he had masked throughout his life. Somehow, without any scientific proof, I sensed he had been lifted out of his darkness. He was put on mood stabilizers and fought to find himself again. Medications lifted him out of psychosis, but it was a long, harrowing struggle. Fortunately, Frank was away during this period, having taken a teaching post in Bologna, Italy. I promised to keep him informed and felt I could manage better alone. I looked after my son through a terrible time when Phil saw electricity coming out of outlets and shuffled like a zombie with the other zombies out for a communal walk.

Thorazine was the medication of choice in the Seventies. I met with the doctor, took the train to White Plains every Saturday, listened as Phil begged me to get him out of there. It was harrowing, and I was afraid he would remain psychotic. With the help of the social service staff upon admission, Phil was able to receive Medicaid benefits that paid for the hospital cost of $10,000 a month. Without Medicaid and SSI, Phil would have been transferred from Bellevue to Manhattan State for we could not have afforded the cost.

One afternoon, we sat in the dayroom together. I had brought Phil's favorite sandwich, roast beef on a roll with Russian dressing. There had been a dramatic improvement. Perhaps it was the mood stabilizer or just healing and time. Phil dreamed once more of being free in the wind and sunlight, and as he spoke, his face was bright with happiness. Yes, my Phil had returned, a true miracle. Sadly, his addiction problems were never addressed, but then, it seemed enough that he had recovered from madness and was determined to stay away from all drugs. I had researched a safe haven where Phil could continue to get better. We received permission to visit Gould Farm in Massachusetts, a residence for post-hospitalization recovery. Phil had an interview, and we looked around. That I was able to make my own decisions regarding Phil's aftercare made the transition easier. Phil was discharged and agreed to live at Gould Farm, where he remained for six months. He was gradually weaned off medication. This was their philosophy. Phil healed, but slowly over many years. He was not without demons, and he struggled. I believe he attended Narcotic Anonymous meetings once in a while, but not enthusiastically. I knew this was something that could only come from him, and I stayed out of it. Phil did not require further hospitalization and he remained drug free, to the best of my knowledge, for close to nine years without needing to take psychiatric medication. Then everything changed.

SIX

The Kitchen

It was 1991. Spring arrived and the scent of blossoms and a river breeze drifted once again through the open windows of my Riverside Drive apartment. I thought about how happy I had felt earlier that morning. I rode my bike to Battery Park along the Hudson River path, emptied of bikers and skaters because it was a weekday. Close to my ritual resting place at the 23rd Street pier, I had taken off my helmet to let the wind play with my waist-length silver and brown braid. I pedaled top speed to reach my destination, eager to find the best bench, determined not only by privacy but also by how directly the sun would make contact with my body. Bike parked, I peeled off my shirt, under which I wore a scant, cotton, sleeveless top for maximum sun exposure. How good to stretch out, head on backpack as the sun's energy caressed me. I thought, "My bones are smiling!" as I sank into a meditative silent place. All I could hear was the mournful song of gulls in harmony with the swoosh of river traffic. Small boats and kayaks brought tiny waves to pulse against the pier. Momentarily, I was in a place without words or time. Then, abruptly brought back by the sound of voices, I knew it was time to pedal again. At Battery Park, I turned around to ride home to 78th Street.

The phone rang. I saw Phil's number on the screen. My body tightened, a familiar response to Phil's calls. I answered, my voice calm and cheerful. I did not want him to pick up the worried edge in my voice. Was he using again? Why did I have to be so careful? I knew I had no control over whether Phil did or did not use drugs, or how he lived his life generally. Then, I heard his voice on the phone, "Mom, hey, how ya doing? Listen, what's going on tonight? You want your favorite son over for dinner? Are you missing me?" He's all right, I thought. I could tell by the energy of his voice.

Phil's key was in the door a few minutes past six. He flew into my kitchen with such life and charm. He was now thirty-one. I stretched out my arms for a hug. He wore those strange moon-shaped, tiny psychedelic sunglasses too small for his face. It was odd to see my eyes reflected in his glasses as I wrapped my arms around him. I loved the way he placed the glasses on his wild dark curls that reached his shoulders. He had inherited my hair and his father's intense, brown eyes. Phil tossed his jean jacket carelessly on a chair. "I'm starving," he said and leaned down to place a peck on my cheek. Phil began to make the rounds of my apartment, as if to rediscover the feel of home. In the front of the apartment off a long entrance hallway was a room that had once belonged to his sister, Lydia.

He shouted to me in the kitchen. "It's a good guest room now, Mom. How is Lydia by the way? I haven't seen her in ages." I thought it a good sign that he asked about his sister, that he showed interest. How I measured every word he spoke! How careless I had been with our time together, as if we had all the time in the world! It never occurred to me then that I would outlive my son.

Moments later, I walked into the living room to see Phil stare out of the open window, his back to me. In this room, family and friends had gathered for birthday celebrations, parties, dinners, Thanksgivings, and renewal of friendships. I had moved here from Washington Square with my children in 1981, three years after my divorce from Frank. Meanwhile, Phil's addictions and psychiatric problems had a life of their own. I did not know then how completely powerless I was, convinced for years that I could "do something."

A heavy oak table opposite the window held family photos, a small wooden Buddha, and a vase of dried roses. When open, the table could seat twelve for dinner. The room was large enough for my beloved Baldwin baby grand and a small spinet for occasional two piano interludes. Phil spun around to face me. "I'm glad to be here Mom, I've been down the last couple of days." I masked my fear that Phil's depressions would lead him back into drugs. What could I do? Inwardly I was tortured, but I changed the subject and said, "A good meal is just what you need. Lamb chops and baked cauliflower—your favorites!"

Baked cauliflower had been one of my mother's German specialties. When our children were young, we would drive to Bayside for dinner with my parents. On our arrival, my father would greet us at the door. I remember the smile on his face, an apron tied around his rotund belly declaring, "GRANDPA, BEST COOK." He always had a bar of German chocolate for each child. My father liked to pretend he had forgotten as Phil, Dan, and Lydia waited impatiently. Then, without warning, the chocolate would appear, retrieved from the special cabinet only he had access to. My father cooked sauerbraten and spaetzle, a specialty of Ulm. On occasion he surprised us with a roast goose served with dumplings and red cabbage. A family tradition had been goose fat with pieces of goose liver, on fresh rye bread with a pinch of salt. We fought for the largest piece of liver. Our family was all together then.

I completed the final preparations for supper. I loved my old-fashioned kitchen, with its high ceilings and prints of Venice and Paris on the walls. Taped on the refrigerator were slogans left over from the Sixties: "Make Love Not War" and "Spring Mobilization for Peace." They were interspersed between children's drawings yellowed with time, old lists, messages, a 1970 March on Washington poster. I was still a perpetual hippie flower-child at age fifty-six. In the corner of the kitchen, a table covered with a red and white-checkered tablecloth was set for supper. I lit two tall, red candles. On the wall at the far end of the table was my most favorite lamp, a gift from Phil.

I remember the day Phil gave me the lamp. He had come home from school flushed with excitement, holding a package carefully wrapped in newspaper. He handed it to me as his lips curled into a wide grin. I unwrapped the paper carefully to see his precious gift, a lamp he had made for me in shop class. The fish-shaped base had four tiny hooks to hold keys. A pale yellow shade accented with green and red flowers has remained intact. I have kept the lamp where it hangs to this day in the kitchen of my log house.

Dinner was ready. Phil walked over to the table, sat down, and opened a can of Dr. Pepper. I poured myself a glass of Chianti.

"Mom. I'm recording a tape with my band. We found a great singer. We're playing Blackbird, your favorite." Phil began to fiddle with the diamond stud in his left ear. He had surprised me with that earring a few days after he had moved into his East Village apartment, three years earlier. We had found a wonderful fourth floor walkup at 145 Sullivan Street, and Phil had fallen instantly in love with the little studio with a garden view. Phil had been clean for several years. He used money left to him by his grandparents to buy the apartment, and I had provided the rest. It was a wonderful time, full of hope and excitement. My son insisted that he sign a legal IOU as he wanted my portion to be a loan. I was proud and confident he would follow through. For some time, he did pay back small amounts every month.

I cleared the food when Phil sat straight up in his chair and put both hands on the table. When the children were young, Frank and I knew that hands on table would be followed with a bold and forceful "I have an announcement to make." This was a way our children received our undivided attention when they had something to tell us. I smiled to myself. Phil remained silent.

"Let's have some tea," I said as I put the kettle on. Tea was our special after-dinner thing. "Dessert?" I asked, and placed his favorite chocolate pudding with whipped cream in front of him. Phil picked up the spoon, waved it around in slow motion figure eights before it landed on the floor.

I sat down, looked directly at his face and felt a pool of sweat trickle down the palm of my hands onto my skirt. My thoughts knew well how to spin my anxiety into a tornado inside my head. It did not take much. The familiar spin of words went something like this: Phil is less depressed or more depressed. He is okay or not okay. He's using or he's not using. I hated to be so anxious about his emotional states. I didn't really know what they were. I was constantly in his face to quell my own anxiety. I had to mind my own business, let Phil figure out his life. Next I heard his words still so clearly etched in my sad memory.

"I snorted heroin, Mom, just a try, no big deal. It was only once." His casual words lacked emotion, as if he had just told me he had been to the movies. I could not look up but heard myself say, "Do you want more tea?"

Things went downhill from there. The apartment Phil loved soon became a haven for drug users. His addict friends slept in the hall, burned candles, and frightened tenants. The apartment below was water-damaged due to Phil's reckless behavior. I received an eviction notice and cried at Families Anonymous (a twelve-step tough love program for parents of addicted children). I was overwhelmed, confused, and full of anxiety—not to forget, I was also responsible for all damages as a joint owner of the apartment. One day when I knew Phil was not home, I arranged to change the locks. The program had encouraged me to create a situation whereby Phil could hit his own bottom. I felt guilty and was never sure it was the right thing to do. I did not know if hitting bottom was simply a metaphor for overdose and death. Still, it was a risk I decided to take.

Many years later, Lydia told me she would never allow her daughters to be homeless for any reason. A part of me agrees with her. At the time I had felt I had no choice, although I had taken the action with ambivalence. It never would have occurred to me to force my own child into homelessness.

Phil was furious with me and begged me to allow him back into the apartment. He had neither awareness of the damage he had created nor of the havoc drugs caused him. When I looked at Phil's apartment the day I locked him out, I found he had sold everything he held dear. His large TV was no longer on the table. His guitars, speakers, and acoustic equipment were gone. Not so long ago, Phil had been a songwriter and guitarist, on the cusp of some success. Then he took that fateful snort of heroin. He had friends, lovers, and gigs to perform. On a roll, his life had finally pulled together. Now in his apartment, filthy clothes were strewn about and dishes were piled in the sink. The little studio of hope existed no more.

Late one night during the summer of 1993, Phil arrived at my door. I agreed to let him stay the night. A street life of drugs was hard for the son of a refugee from Nazi Germany, as it would be for anyone. Late the next afternoon, Phil walked through the kitchen on his way out the door. "Yo Mom, see ya later " His words prompted me to look up from the bills I had been paying. I barely recognized the person passing through. Phil's silver shapeless pants were threadbare in some places. Glue-like stuff stiffened his spiked hair. His face was pale, and his skinny frame shocked me for a moment, a caricature of the Phil I had once known. He wore a black tee shirt, sleeves cut off, his cross dangling on a long chain around his neck. Old Pumas with holes covered his sockless feet. Pieces of mangled, ratty tail had been tied together and swished around his bony frame, twice around his neck, across the chest and wrapped around his waist. A leftover piece of tail trailed after him. Its former life had been a gray, matted, cotton boa retrieved from a garbage pail in Washington Square Park. He's wearing a dead mongrel, I thought. Who is this weird one who walks past me? It was hard to see.

Phil, his silver pants, and ragged mongrel had become one. He never took them off. "I'm going out to play some guitar," he announced. With his last precious acoustic instrument, he slammed the door behind him and did not return until morning. "What happened to your guitar? Where were you all night?" My anxiety was not to be contained, for I was wild with fear. Who was this man, my former son? The sockets of his tired eyes sunk deeply into his face, bloodshot and vacant. The pitch of my voice rose. "Phil, what has happened?"

"Mom, I walked to the World Trade Center. The buildings are so beautiful, so tall and powerful. I love the World Trade Center, Mom." I looked down at his blackened shoeless feet. "It was beautiful, Mom. God was there."

"Where's your guitar, Phil?" I knew how much he loved his instrument.

"I gave it to a guy at the World Trade Center. He asked to borrow it and swore he would give it back in a few days. He'll give it back,

Mom." Phil did not live long enough to see the 9/11 destruction of his beloved World Trade Center. It would take another three years from that infamous night of the heroin snort to a steady downward spiral that would lead him to the end.

On the morning of March 6, 1996, the Bellevue Hospital morgue was a gray, lifeless place, the smell of death everywhere. Metallic officials gave us forms to sign, to verify Phil's identity. They were robotic people, unsympathetic, cold as the room we stood in. I was about to see my son for the last time on a slab in the morgue. How could it be? I would have wanted to be with Phil at the end, to have helped him pass from the physical to the spirit world. I would have wanted to sit with him, gently touch his head to feel the vibrations of his life as they left his earthly body. I would have wanted to comfort him. When Phil died, he was alone, and there was no goodbye. We stood together in the large room of death, we who loved him so much. Frank, accompanied by his wife, was inconsolable. Daniel stood close and gave me comfort. He too had not said goodbye to his brother, and there was so much left unsaid.

Throughout the years, Dan had suffered from the loss of his brother-turned-addict. He had turned away from Phil, unable to tolerate his crazy and self-destructive behavior. Lydia, the youngest of my three children, had not yet returned from a vacation that had been interrupted so cruelly by the news of her brother's death on the same day as her birthday. Lydia lost not only her brother but also an uncle for her young daughter, Melina.

Wild with grief, ghosts of our past hovered about as if to warm the frozen room. Lilli and Fritz; Frank's parents, Clae and Herb; aunts and uncles; my sister Carol.

Alone with Phil for the last time, I saw his face behind the glass partition. We were painfully separate. I could neither touch him nor run my fingers through his beautiful, dark curls, cropped short. I wanted to study his face, to memorize each detail, to touch the dark eyebrows, familiar and loved. Long lashes fell onto his cheek. His eyes were at rest. He could have been asleep, relaxed, despite my awareness that an unauthorized autopsy had been performed, for which I would have not given permission had I been asked. I would not have wanted his body to be mutilated, cut open under the white sheet that covered him to his chin. I did not need to read that his organs and heart were that of a healthy thirty-six-year-old male. I knew he had ingested drugs. I did not need to read how much alcohol was found. I did not want to see my son for the last time behind the sterile glass partition of a morgue. What had driven him to go back into the world of drugs? Did he want to die? Was it suicide? The thought had come up for me many times. Yet, I didn't think so. Phil had told me often how much he loved life.

I felt the cold in my veins permeate through me as I shivered uncontrollably and slid into panic, my breath under siege. It was all too much. I could do no more than breathe: In-breath light, out-breath pain. I could do no more than be with truth. Phil was dead and I had to live on, one breath at a time. I wonder how parents of children brutalized and unnaturally killed in desperate wars—in Palestine, Germany, or anywhere in the world—could live through such grief. I am now one with them, and this gives me strength.

I dreamed I walked through a snowstorm with no visibility. As I searched for Phil in the bleak winter starless night, a light shone through the storm. I followed it until I found Phil, encased in a slab of ice.

I was alone in a massive room dominated by a marble wall at the former Terezenstadt concentration camp in the Czech Republic. I was reminded that I was a Jew. I could have been one more name on the interminable lists of children exterminated by the Nazis between 1941 and 1945. These lists of names were on the wall, covered with glass. I had been one breath away from extermination. My eyes were wet and filled with grief and guilt for having survived. Hovering over me were ghosts of dead children and my son.

I carried this image with me. My refugee background and my beloved son's drug overdose became mired in confusion and difficult to sort out. Who was I? American? German? Jewish? What was my own destiny and what did I believe? How could I go on? Phil's death, combined with the end of a nine-year relationship with a man I had loved deeply, plunged me into a black abyss, a major depression last-ing seven months.

In that dark place, my own daughter hardly recognized the blank face that stared back at her. Two major losses contributed to another difficult period of my life. A paralysis of spirit came over me in the form of exhaustion, lack of motivation or hope, and a de-sire to escape through sleep. But sleep did not come easily, for the darkness was accompanied by anxiety, nausea, and a restless panic. Without warning, I awoke with palpitations, profuse sweating, fa-tigue, and no appetite. My body ached. Convinced I was having a heart attack, I scheduled a stress test with a cardiologist who gave me a clean bill of health. I continued to feel lost, rootless, unmo-tivated, hopeless, and deeply depressed. Each day was worse than the last. Unable to eat, I lost weight. My fear that I would become psychotic like my mother and the history of depression and suicides in my family, drove me to a psychiatrist who prescribed a course of antidepressants. Some Ativan that I cut into quarters gave me two or three hours of sleep. I did not want to wake up. I never thought I would take these medications and now was grateful for the brief relief. I began to see a grief counselor who had little impact. Only Zoloft eventually lifted me back to myself, but it took months. My head felt stuffed with cotton. Dreadful feelings of being alone scared me. I could not connect with anyone or make sense of what was happening.

I thought of impermanence, moment-to-moment changes. I tried deep breathing. I meditated and finally decided to reach out to a *sangha* friend. For several summers I had attended a week-long workshop, "Unconditional Presence," for psychotherapists who practiced meditation. At Omega Institute in Rhinebeck, New York, about seventy-five of us would gather for one week to meditate and reflect. This became our *sangha*, our little Buddhist communi-ty. I especially loved the three days we meditated and remained in silence. I would spend many weekends in the coming years medi-tating in silence at various Buddhist retreats. Learning how to be in the moment, while completely aware of what was coming and going in my mind as well as outside stimuli, taught me how to find stillness in myself. It has been an invaluable teaching. Still it was of no help in the darkness of my anxiety and depression. It was then I decided to email a friend from the *sangha* who was himself able to heal from his major depressions. I needed to find hope, and he provided strength in his directives for me to stay on my medication when I felt like going off, work out at the gym even for five minutes, and take steam baths in order to sweat. He promised recovery, but told me to be patient. I was in real distress and thought I could not withstand it. One day, I took myself to the gym twenty blocks away and lasted about five minutes. On my way home, as the #5 bus on Broadway pulled up to the curb, I rushed to the opened door. My legs buckled and I fell smack on my stomach alongside the curb. Dazed, I cried out for help. People gathered at the bus stop ignored me. I held my arm out for assistance. The callous indifference brought to my consciousness an aspect of New York I had not known before. Someone finally pulled me up and helped me onto the bus. Disconnect and fear at the bus stop provided a moment of clarity. The callous indifference would propel me in a few months' time to sell my apartment and move out of the city to be closer to nature, trees, and quiet.

I believe it is with strength and determination that I found myself again with a renewed life force, gratitude, and joy. On reflection, the entire period was one more of life's lessons, and it ultimately propelled me into action.

PART TWO

SEVEN
Israel

The activism I participated in against the Vietnam War, for women's rights, against the South African apartheid regime, and against the war in Iraq and subsequent U.S. military intervention was powered by the action and leadership of others. Of course I felt passion, but my role was as a follower, not a leader. I took part in rallies others had organized. I was not driven to organize, stand up, and speak out as an individual but was more comfortable as part of a collective, a community of protesters. I felt safe in that role. No one personally attacked me for my beliefs or labeled me anti-Semitic. To be "unpatriotic" suited me, for it symbolized opposition to wars, to our military-industrial complex, and to the belief in intervention or "democratization" as a means to acquire of natural resources and strategic power in the Middle East. If patriotism was equated with support of wars and global superiority, I wanted no part of it.

I took my first trip to Israel in the early 1970s, where I met for the first time my extended Lebrecht family. In the beginning, disengaged from Israeli politics, I was in love with the collective ways of life. I loved the land and its beauty. I had bought the myth of Israel as the only democracy in the Middle East. I had heard the story of a barren desert brought to life by Jews, who had come there to build a Jewish homeland. For the first time, I felt a strong identification and pride as a Jew, safe and protected from anti-Semitism. They were good visits then, rare times when I still loved the idea of Israel and wanted to believe with all my heart that Jews could be free from persecution and Israel could be a beacon of light to shine on the world following a long history of darkness and despair. However, it is important to say, I was never a Zionist, for I am opposed to any form of nationalism.

My own awareness of problems within Israel developed slowly, steadily, and with a heavy heart, for I live with memories that identify with refugees, all refugees made homeless by nationalism. As a child who miraculously survived one of the most heinous, racist crimes of the twentieth century, I was determined to attempt to understand without bias the Palestinian-Israeli story, which encompasses an intertwined narrative of profound suffering on both sides. Both stories are about oppression, victimization, and struggles against annihilation. Both stories are about untold refugees who have lost their homes and their lives. I have heard said there is only one true narrative. Israel has created its own narrative to justify the Zionist dream to be a Jewish State only.

Some members of the Lebrecht family had emigrated to South America—Chile and Brazil. My second cousin, Edmundo Lebrecht, grew up in Chile. After Pinochet and his fascist crowd seized power in 1973, he was arrested and tortured. Edmundo was detained in a concentration camp but later was released with the help of Hans Lebrecht. He was then deported to Germany where he spent several years in exile, first in Ulm and then Berlin. He returned to Chile after the fall of Pinochet. I pay tribute to Edmundo, a freedom fighter. He died recently at the age of sixty-eight.

In the United States, I had two first cousins, of whom one recently died, the children of my father's sister, Grete Moos. Their grandchildren remain scattered about, including a daughter and grandson who live in Israel. My cousins and their children have distanced themselves from me since learning I was a passenger on the Jewish Boat to Gaza in 2010. They strongly disapproved and were outraged for I had "betrayed my Jewish heritage and was a traitor to Israel." Nothing is further from the truth. To dissent is not to betray what it means to be Jewish. According to Molly Ivens, a liberal newspaper columnist and humorist from Texas whom I greatly admired, "Dissent is what rescues democracy from a quiet death behind closed doors." Most important, to dissent is *not* to be anti-Semitic.

I met Alexander (Karl) and Elisheva Neumeyer in 1976. Karl was a cousin of my grandmother, Gisela Lebrecht. In Germany, he had studied law but chose instead to learn farming, which became his life's work. They were Zionists, and to embrace Judaism was an important part of their life. Karl and Elisheva had left Germany for Argentina before Kristallnacht, where they founded with four friends a very primitive collective farm in Avigdor, some distance from Buenos Aires. Three children, Manuel (Immanuel), Miguel (Micha), and Judith were born there. Eventually Avigdor was too isolated to raise their children, and in Karl's words, "During our stay in Argentina, we became convinced that the Jewish people will have a future only by realizing the ideas of Zionism." He wrote to friends in Israel, and the family was invited to come directly to Shavei Tzion (Zion/freedom). Their last daughter, Esti, was born soon after.

I was eager to meet them and curious to know about the collective way of life. A community of families who lived and worked together, had childcare and a communal structure appealed to me enormously. *Moshav* is the Hebrew word for "settlement," a type of cooperative agricultural community generally based on the principle of private ownership of land, as opposed to *kibbutzim*, which has no private ownership.

Shavei Tzion stands adjacent to the Mediterranean Sea, south of Nahariya. Karl wrote, "From the first day at Shavei Tzion, we were enchanted by the beauty of the place. On one side the Mediterranean, on the other the view of the Galilee mountains where villages shone with the glow of the setting sun and pretty homes stood surrounded by green and colorful gardens." I was completely enamored with their family life in painful contrast to my early life in Bayside. Perhaps I also idealized Karl and his gentle ways, so inviting and generous, and their simple house in which I met the entire family many times for sumptuous, festive meals. They exuded joy and simplicity, a down-to-earth charm and a visible contentment. Elisheva carried herself without the slightest vanity. She was heavy-set and embodied the kind of mother I had dreamed of but lacked in my own life. She took me under her wing with warmth and exuberance. There was no criticizing, no discontent. I loved them. So full of life and hope, their children produced twelve grandchildren who, as far as I know, all served in the Israeli army. They were content in this land, and why not? They lived good, productive lives and thought of themselves as pioneers. All the children eventually left the *moshav*, for the collective life of their parents no longer interested them. Many second-generation children abandoned life in the *kibbutzim* and *moshavim*.

I visited Yad Vashem in Jerusalem. Stone engravings outside the house of pain listed some of the camps: Sobidor, Treblinka, Dachau, Majdanek, Auschwitz-Osweichem, Chelmno, Drancy, Lwow-Janowska, Belzec, Mauthausen, Klooga, Jasenovac, Stutthof, Theresiensstadt. The names evoke horror and raise the eternal question: in the name of humanity, how could human beings inflict so much brutality upon one another? I walked through the children's memorial, a vast hall of grief that documented 1,600,000 murdered children. One can only weep to see photographs of all our children mounted on an endless wall, accompanied by the music of death in the background; 1,600,000 candles reflected eerily on the ceiling from one burning candle. I gasped and recognized again the joy and pain of survival. As each child's name, age, and country of origin was called out, I questioned the reason I was spared and my purpose for living. I left Yad Vashem shaken and could only hear the words, "never again."

The most influential and beloved relative I met in Israel was a first cousin of my father, also born in Ulm, Germany. Hans Lebrecht became my mentor. He was a progressive humanist who fought for freedom and justice. Hans showed me another face of Israel. He had been an active resistance fighter in World War II, a noted Communist activist and journalist who later withdrew from the party. Hans, along with Uri Avnery, an Israeli writer also born also to a well-established German Jewish family, founded the Gush Shalom peace movement ("The Peace Bloc") in 1993. Avnery had been a member of the Irgun as a teenager and sat in the Knesset from 1965–74 and 1979–81. He and Hans were friends and colleagues. The aim of Gush Shalom has been to achieve peace and reconciliation with the Palestinian people and to put an end to the occupation.

Hans was the father I wanted: a human rights activist, intellectual, mentor. I loved him and will always miss his lively intellect and

Hans Lebrecht in Ramallah, 1992.

commitment to peace and justice. He had lived in Kibbutz Beit Oren
and died in September 2014, at age ninety-nine. Formerly he and his
life partner Tosca lived in Tel Aviv, where I visited them often. In
2001, Hans sent a New Year's letter to all his friends and relatives
with the following greeting that imparts the essence of who he was:

121

"For everyone a year in the best possible health, a year that sees an end to all wars, xenophobia, fascism, hunger and poverty on earth—a year of success on the path towards socialism, true democracy, and equality for all, towards genuine, just, and lasting peace. Jerusalem, Capital of Two States—Only Way to Peace." In that time, it was still possible to consider a two-state solution.

I recall well my father's words to me: "Hans is the black sheep of the family." His left-socialist philosophy, his participation in a communist-led underground movement, as well as his role as a resistance fighter raised questions from his more mainstream family members who were not politically active. I feel proud to have also become the "black sheep" of whatever small family is left. I was intrigued from the outset before I had even met him. Hans spent his life active in the development of the peace front in Israel and Palestine. In June 1992, there had been hope in Israel. Labor had won the Israeli elections. Rabin, known to be have been a military hawk, pledged to stop building settlements in the West Bank and Gaza. Meretz, the left-wing Zionist socialist democratic party, had won twelve seats, and five seats were won by the Arab parties in the Knesset. Then, in 1995, Rabin was assassinated by a Jewish fanatic. Now in 2015, Jewish right-wing fanaticism has grown, as thugs threaten and harm the left-wing Israeli community. As Hans once predicted, it is "Jew against Jew" that has morphed into a dangerous threat, united no more.

Peace has not been a viable alternative. I had so many questions as I became aware of the two faces of Israel. How was it possible that Israelis were able to build a socialist form of communal living on someone else's land? It did not make sense.

In 1992, Hans and I visited Birzeit, a Palestinian town north of Ramallah in the central West Bank. We had lunch in the home of Abbas Abdul-Haq, his German-born wife Ursula, and their four children. Abbas, a large, rotund, friendly man of about fifty, was at the time a Palestinian engineering professor at Birzeit University, the first Palestinian university. This was the first time I heard how Israeli soldiers appeared without warning to search homes, mostly in the middle of the night, in order to check for terrorists and weapons.

Demolished houses, ghosts of their former selves, stood naked and abandoned, adding to the stark surroundings of a war zone. Where had the families gone? What happened to Abbas and his family? I felt the pain of another time: the Nazification of Germany, the victims of the Nazi dictatorship who were forced to leave their homes. Now in the year 2014, when I hear the commonly used term "Judaization of Israel," I cringe.

In Birzeit, beautiful stone houses stood, built with multiple levels to accommodate multiple families. It had not occurred to me that Palestinian houses must be built upward for lack of land space. In comparison, sprawling areas of new settlements arose across the hills, where flourishing Jewish communities would, within several decades, swallow up Palestinian land, farms, and former homes. Where I stood as I entered the garden of our Birzeit hosts, a steel fence like prison gates provided an illusion of safety. Inside the garden, flowers bloomed alongside fruit trees. In contrast, streets were dust and stone, neglected and barren—demolished stone, for me, a dreadful sight. The illusion of safety behind steel gates belied the reality of Israeli soldiers who would come knocking and enter at their pleasure at any moment of any dark night. As I looked across the hilltops beyond, no wall had yet separated "them and us." As I stood there in the 1970s, I was shocked with a sense of existential dread for which I had yet no logical understanding.

That day in Birzeit, Abbas's wife Ursula spoke of "Israeli soldiers who behave like Nazis." I listened with disbelief, for I could not accept a comparison between Israelis and Nazis. I was confused and terribly upset. As I listened, she said, "No one harbors anti-Semitic feelings against Jews. There is hatred toward the Zionist agenda against Palestinian rights." For the first time I heard this distinction spoken by Palestinians. It would become a crucial distinction in my understanding of the Israeli government. It would also take years to digest and assimilate, this necessity to separate out Jew from Zionist. They are not one. Nationalist Zionists are not the same as non-Zionist Jews. Some Zionist Jews see themselves as post-Zionist. In my

Hans and Lillian, 1993.

view, a person who is supportive of a *heimat*, a Jewish State only for Jews, is a Zionist and opposes equal rights for Jews and Palestinians.

Disturbed by Ursula's pronouncement, I had insisted at the time Israelis could never be compared to Nazis. It seemed preposterous then to make this comparison. The monsters of German Nationalism could not be alive in Israel. Israel was still a country I wanted to love. Ursula continued to speak of the occupation, stolen land, bulldozed homes, soldiers who entered homes in the middle of the night, frightened families, crying children, the search for terrorists.

During another visit with Hans, Ursula made us a wonderful Palestinian lunch, including two types of stuffed grape leaves, stuffed zucchini, lamb and rice with slivered almonds, and a delicious thistle root vegetable only found in that area. Abbas had come home from teaching for a one-hour rest period. After lunch, we sat in the garden surrounded by barbed wire on a beautiful sunny day. As Ursula began to speak, she told a frightening story. It was several weeks ago, she said, after a bus blew up. At 10 p.m., a truck drove up and down the road with bright flashing lights and a loud speaker. As it passed their house, they heard their names on the loudspeaker. The family had no idea what was going on. Ursula called up the mayor for information and help. Then, a loud bang on the door: "Open up. Everyone out of the house." The young kids were sleeping, and they were afraid. I can't help but be reminded of another time when Nazi's broke into the homes of Jews to round up, arrest, or search them.

They opened the door after several moments of loud banging. Soldiers came in with rifles. The whole family was forced to stand outside, very still without moving while the soldiers searched for weapons. What was happening? They had no idea. Ursula thought at any moment they would be killed. The soldiers went into the house and turned everything upside down. Later, I suppose prompted by the mayor, who arrived on the scene because Abbas and Ursula were known in Beir Zeit, a soldier apologized. It seems Abbas's house had been suspected to have hidden a "terrorist" after the Israeli bus was blown up. Since then, apologies are unknown and soldiers have permission to search, demolish, and enter at will Palestinian homes and to terrorize, kill, and drag to prison without charge Palestinians (including children).

Ursula spoke of her plan to take the children to Germany. I struggled for the next four decades to understand Zionism and Judaism as distinct and separate entities.

You may wonder how Hans and I were able to drive in and out of occupied Palestine at that time. It was not easy, for Birzeit was a hotbed for terrorist activity. Abbas had been imprisoned twice. Hans had put a foreign press sign, written in Arabic, on his windshield. This did not always work, he said, because press cards were known to be used to spy. At one point, Hans got lost as we were driving back to Tel Aviv. Visibly anxious, he would not ask directions from an Israeli soldier as they could not be trusted, and questions would arouse too much suspicion.

Something important changed for me as a result of my visits. The myth of Israel as a "beacon of light" to the world was shattered permanently. It has been a painful awareness for me as a Jew and refugee. The pain is not about a dream of Zionism and a Jewish safe haven, for I was never a Zionist. Instead it is the horrible truth that Jews, once victims of a monstrous "Final Solution," would reinvent themselves as racist victimizers in order to realize the dream of a safe haven for Jews only. For many years, I still tried to defend Israel. I know now my reactions were in response to emotions that were linked amorphously to the "Final Solution." I was not yet ready to explore two separate entities, Judaism and nationalistic Zionism or their relationship to Israel.

Hans introduced me to friends from Gush Shalom and other peace movements. I heard another story, the Palestinian narrative, the story of the Nakba, or "catastrophe" in Arabic. My fear of nationalism in all forms deepened, and I now understand we must cultivate a capacity to empathize with our "enemy" in consideration of our common human condition if we are to break the cycle of endless wars and destruction. To develop empathy must be learned for too often empathy in nationalist societies has been replaced with learned racism and hatred.

As I toured Israel with Hans as my guide, I observed a visible yet subtle "attitude" toward Sephardic Jews, those Jews originally expelled from Spain, who contrasted with the "cultivated" Askanazi Jews from Western Europe. I had picked up racism. I had not expected this in my naïve idealization of Israel and felt disturbed. Questions of race and attitudes emerged in my consciousness. Because of my new awareness, I would be told I was anti-Israel. The truth is, if Israel and Palestine could coexist together, I would be a proud Jew.

EIGHT

The Jewish Boat

For many years between 1991 and 2008, I was lucky to travel around the world to remote places still untouched by Western development. I journeyed to the Amazon, Iquitos, Pucallpa, and found small tribes along the Peruvian Amazon during a time when logging had not yet devastated the area. Within a decade, I had visited Borneo, Thailand, India, Nepal, Burma, Irian Jaya (Western New Guinea), Bali, Vietnam, Laos, and Cambodia. Over and over again, I was drawn to Asia, hungry for the culture and its people. I trekked to indigenous, poverty-stricken villages and used a Polaroid camera—first to engage the children, then quickly the whole village. Although we had no access to a common verbal language, through our eyes and body language the borders of differences seemed to melt away for brief periods. They were unique moments as I discovered a common thread between us, fragile but alive, full of compassion, interest, curiosity, and yes, love. I could not get enough. I know that beneath skin surfaces and cultural differences, we are all connected on a deep level that brings us truly to our humanity.

It was after this period of travel and discovery that I embarked on the most significant adventure of my life. It all began on June 17, 2010, when a friend sent me an article written by Adam Horowitz and published on the news website *Mondoweiss*:

> It seems the Jewish boat attempting to break the siege of Gaza has struck a nerve. Organizers are looking for a second boat due to overwhelming demand. From *Haaretz: An association of German Jews planning to send a boat to break the Gaza blockade is searching for a second vessel, given the high number of requests to travel with the group."*

The group from Germany, Jewish Voice for a Just Peace (Judische Stimme) originally planned to send one vessel from an undisclosed

Mediterranean port in July, with the aim of getting past the Israeli-imposed blockade of Gaza.

Without a moment's thought and inexplicably driven, I knew I had to find the organizers and contact them. I found Edith Lutz and Kate Leiterer, the original German organizers and wrote to them. In my search, I stumbled across other sites: American Jews for Just Peace and Jewish Voice for Peace in Oakland, California. They helped me to locate Edith and Kate, and I became aware that day I was no longer isolated.

Here is what I wrote:

> I am a refugee from Nazi Germany (Frankfurt), human rights activist, poet, writer and psychoanalyst. I have traveled around the world, including Germany and Israel (have relatives there). Other German Jews, mostly elderly relatives, as well as American Jews in all areas but Israel, many of whom are progressive, are in complete disagreement with me. As a Jew and particularly as a German Jew, I feel a commitment to equal human rights for everyone. 'Never again' has deep personal significance and requires that I not only speak out but take action against injustice and human rights abuses. I am painfully aware of a growing split in Israel between Likud and Labor, a split that divides the country and has become increasingly violent within the two factions of the Jewish community. My uncle Hans Lebrecht (now over 90), formerly from Ulm, predicted this two decades ago. I have been with him many times in Israel, and it was he who first introduced me to Palestinian families, his friends in the West Bank. I met families I grew to love in the years we continued our friendship. I would like to be a passenger on this boat in an effort to break the blockade and to end Israel's siege. I speak fluent German, although my ability to read is better in English. How can I make this happen? Awaiting your reply.
>
> Lillian Rosengarten (formerly Gisela Lillian Lebrecht)

On June 19, 2010, I was invited to join the Jewish Boat to Gaza. I was given a gift of great magnitude that would change my life, for I would find my voice as an advocate for Palestinian justice. The organizers were in communication with the U.S. and Israeli governments in an attempt to guarantee safe passage for the Jewish boat and to permit entry into Gaza to accomplish its peaceful and humanitarian efforts. As I prepared to leave at a moment's notice, I knew this was exactly what I needed to do. I was determined, without hesitation and without comprehending why the forces that guided me in this decision were so strong. My daughter Lydia begged me not to go. "There are so many other things you can do from here," she pleaded. Her agitated self was afraid. "You put yourself at risk, Mom. You could die." Later in a phone interview with the *New York Times* on September 28, 2010, Lydia said, "I was reluctant to see her go out of my own anxiety, but I find myself incredibly impressed by her bravery." My son Dan more or less accepted my decision as I showered him with articles in attempts to persuade him. Melina and Emilia, my granddaughters, emulated their mother Lydia's fears. When seven-year-old Emi asked, "Omi, are you happy you are going on the ship?" and I responded "Very happy," she gave me permission. "Okay, Omi, you can go." Melina, then sixteen, accepted my decision despite reservations, for she too feared for my safety. Close friends were worried. I understood their concerns but was not deterred.

Why a Jewish boat? It could have been any boat or another form of active resistance. It is important to reiterate again that I am an assimilated Jew with no affiliation to organized religion. Despite that, I am still a Jew. I don't believe in wars and am a pacifist. I believe in dialogue and speaking to the enemy. We must attempt to understand the "other" through active listening and practice empathy through techniques of learning to put oneself in the other person's experience. In my view, it is urgent to engage in conflict resolution through peaceful means. Israel uses violence in an attempt to "conquer" the enemy, resulting in new generations of learned hatred, institutionalized racism, and endless suffering. That it was a "Jewish" boat is significant because of my background, for it provided an opportunity to speak out against human rights abuses as a Jew. I was determined to say to all who would listen, "I am a Jew, and the actions of the Zionist government are not in my name." The Jewish Boat provided me with a vehicle for dissent as we sailed to the place we were warned not to enter.

On September 21, I flew to London, where I stayed in a nearby suburb with Arthur Goodman and his wife for the few days before our departure. Arthur, an organizer, was strict about not divulging information so that our trip would not be sabotaged by the Israeli government. I had no idea where we were going or when we would leave, and naturally this fed a sense of dread I had not experienced before. I had packed lightly and took with me a computer and camera. Until my arrival in London, I had not considered fear as a deterrent from joining the group, for I was too caught up in anticipation to think about what might go wrong. I thought about the diligent notes and photographs I would take. Instead, I left my electronics with Arthur to send back to the United States when I realized they would be confiscated by the Israeli Defense Force (IDF) should we be intercepted.

It was on my arrival in London when fear took over and I began to question what I was doing there. Was I crazy to risk my life? I knew that on May 30, the *Mavi Marmara*, a great Turkish ship and part of the Gaza Freedom Flotilla, had headed to Gaza with activists from many countries on board. I knew the *Mavi* had been ambushed by Israeli Navy forces in the dark of the night by helicopters and frigates. Nine passengers were murdered and many were injured. The Freedom Flotilla had been intended to get past the Israeli blockade, to deliver aid to Gaza, to raise international awareness about the inhumane conditions in Gaza, and to work toward ending sanctions and the occupation. The Free Gaza movement, an international coalition of pro-Palestinian human rights organizations and activists, is endorsed by Desmond Tutu and Noam Chomsky, and includes numerous Jewish groups that campaign for the rights of Palestinians. Israel had vowed to block the flotilla from reaching Gaza and accused the organizers of embarking on "an act of provocation" against the Israeli military. Additionally, they claimed its entry into the twenty nautical mile closure of the sea off Gaza would amount to a violation of international law.

To keep my anxiety at bay, I talked myself into believing the Jewish Boat would remain safe, for no such incident could reoccur. And besides, we were all Jews. Yes, this is how I rationalized our safety.

Arthur was a member of Jews for Justice for Palestine, our London-based sponsor organization. Full credit must be given to Edith Lutz and Kate Leiterer, the original organizers for a German Jewish Boat to Gaza. They met with Glyn Secher in March 2010 and were eager for him to become captain. He agreed, and fortunately for us, they could not have found a more personable and experienced captain. Edith, Kate, and Glyn were originally promised a loan from a socially conscious bank to buy a comfortable sixteen-passenger sailboat. Humble contributions had been made for the purchase. Glyn, a British citizen, was and remains a member of the London-based JFJFP, one of the biggest and most influential organizations campaigning for the end of Israeli occupation of Palestinian territories. In May, as they were inspecting the original sailboat they had hoped to buy, the bank withdrew its support following the *Mavi Marmara* disaster. Glyn's organization, JFJFP London, agreed to take over the rest of the planning and secure a boat as they had more members and were financially stronger. It was Glyn who located a twenty-year-old catamaran, which he refurbished for the voyage. It was named *Irene* in honor of Irene Bruegel, the human rights activist and socialist feminist who had founded JFJFP in 2001 and died in 2008.

Immediately after arriving at Arthur's house, I was aware of a tight level of secrecy required to prevent the Israeli secret police from sabotaging our attempts to reach Gaza. Little information was forthcoming. I knew nothing except we were to be ten people on board, which included four elderly Jewish passengers. The crew were two brothers, Israeli refuseniks formerly recruited into the Israeli navy as pilots. I wondered briefly about my all-too-spontaneous decision to join the group. In my later adult life, I have often seized the moment in a way that may be considered too impulsive, when I make quick decisions based on my intuitive awareness. I know my emotions can propel me into action, and I have learned to trust my instincts, which tend to guide me in the right direction. At times, I have been able to take risks I have not regretted and have learned to respect my intuitive process.

Arthur, a slender, middle-aged man, carried a serious demeanor and paid close attention to every detail of the trip. He had scheduled a meeting with the organization in London that afternoon. His wife, Paula, a more relaxed and very kind woman, took me under her wing. They lived in an attached stone house with a beautiful English garden. It had a European atmosphere I could easily relate to. I remember well their two large, slender, and most unusual, beautiful Lurcher dogs, this breed unfamiliar to me. Arthur left for his meeting in central London, and Paula left to give an art lesson. Arthur's parting words as he rushed out were, "Have you made up your will?" Although meant as a joke, for a moment I took him literally. Left alone, anxiety and exhilaration swept over me in waves as I paced the rooms. I was certain I had made a huge mistake. I had to return home. I called my dear friend, Connie Hogarth, an activist with a fine, level-headed ability to listen and advise. "Connie, I am afraid; I cannot do this," I confided to her. Her words dissipated my panic. "You must do this Lillian, and you want to." I knew she was right, of course. The atmosphere of secrecy had heightened my fear. I had to let go and simply be in the moment.

Two days later, Arthur and I took three trains to Gatwick airport and flew to Istanbul. During our layover, I met other passengers and organizers. I was especially excited to meet Edith Lutz, for it was she who had negotiated my place on the Jewish Boat. Edith would become a most important activist friend. I also met Vanessa, Glyn Secher's wife. She joined us at the hotel in North Cyprus as we waited for the boat to arrive, but she would not be a passenger. There had been a long list of would-be passengers. I did not know until shortly before I left the United States I had been included. Edith said there had been a mix-up when the British organization took over and so many more had wanted to join.

I met Allison Prager, our media coordinator, who would not be a passenger, as she had become ill. That now left nine passengers. Also at the airport was Diana Neslen, executive board member of JFJFP. She was tremendously helpful in her organization and support while we were in Cyprus.

At the hotel in Kyrenia, Turkish Cyprus, I felt a frenetic combination of excitement, waiting, and not knowing when and where the boat would land. I found Turkish Cyprus exotic with few, if any, American tourists. I wrote emails at an internet café and visited an old fort at the entrance of the old city. I explored, sat at a café, and drank cold orange juice. I wrote in my journal (confiscated later by the Israelis) and watched a stream of sweltering tourists pass along. I am the only one here who will sail to Gaza, I thought and felt exhilarated. We will be okay, I rationalized. The Israelis would not dare to hurt us, a small group of Jews in a tiny catamaran. They would not dare hurt us after the murder of nine activists on the big flotilla *Mavi Marmara*. I felt safe with my thoughts, naïve in my belief that Jews would not hurt Jews.

Of course, the other side of my exhilaration was fear. I recall a time when Hans told me during one of my stays in Israel, "You wait, Lillian; it will become the most difficult war of Jew against Jew." His words now reentered my questioning mind as I thought about what constituted a Jew as opposed to an Israeli or a Zionist. How are they all distinct from one another? Would it be Zionist Jews fighting non-Zionist Jews? Would it be a Jewish nationalistic theocracy without separation of church and state against secular (and perhaps more liberal) Jews? Would it be Jews against the illegal occupation fighting Israel's assertion of the "moral righteousness" that dictated land ownership for Jews only? What a distortion to present those who kill as morally righteous! Jew against Jew has sprung forth from an ideology, the pursuit of a Zionist state for Zionists (and Jews?) only or only Zionists if the perception lives that all Jews need to be Zionists to have a true allegiance to Israel. It is disturbing to recognize the increasing discord between all people who choose ideology and wars over dialogue and empathy.

I awaited the arrival of our boat, *Irene*. At the hotel, I met Rami and Reuven, Vish, our London-based photographer, and Eli, an Israeli Channel 10 journalist. Diana oversaw everyone. She and Allyson were in touch with Glyn and the crew. We others were kept in the dark. Arthur warned we were under surveillance by the Israeli secret police. He told us to take the batteries out of our cell phones and to use phone cards for all calls. I missed Lydia and called her, ignoring Arthur's instructions. I bonded with Edith and Vanessa, went swimming, walked the city, and regrouped. The boat would land on Friday at Famagusta port. At one time, between 1946 to 1948, hundreds of Jews were interned in camps by British colonial administrators who ruled Cyprus at the time. They had tried to emigrate to Palestine, then also under British rule.

Irene docked at Famagusta under the guise of a rented tourist boat named *Sven-Y-Two* in order to avoid suspicion. Fortunately, a local fisherman gave us permission to use one of his berths. Famagusta is now under Turkish control, while ports in southern Cyprus are under Greek Cypriot control. These ports had been used to launch Gaza-bound activists from 2000 to 2009 but are now banned by Greek Cypriots. A willing port and safe docking brought relief to our group, and we greeted Glyn, Itamar, and Yonatan with excited hugs. Three marvelous men, competent and a joy to be with. I found them amazing. Coincidentally, I had met Yonatan a year before when he spoke at the Connie Hogarth Center for Social Action at Manhattanville College. He told of Israeli men and women, the "refuseniks," who no longer agreed to serve in the Israeli military. I was as excited then to hear his story as I was now to be traveling with him. Gone was my wavering fear for I knew then I was exactly where I needed to be.

The next morning, a press conference was organized with local AP journalists. The Jewish Boat to Gaza would soon be news around the world. Later that day we had a briefing. Glyn reiterated our commitment to nonviolence and to engage in passive resistance. This meant we would only sail to Gaza and would refuse, if captured, to take the *Irene* to another port.

On Sunday, ready to set sail, we had a surprise that caused concern. As we neared the dock, about to embark, we were greeted by the sight of the police and Glyn. We were told regulations required the police to hold all of our passports. The police seized them, and I wondered if we woud be allowed to leave the port. Fear crept in as it appeared the police had suspected the boat was headed for Gaza despite all the secrecy and the pretense of the *Sven-Yi-Two* being a pleasure boat. Too many journalists had surrounded us, and too much activity had taken place around loading and organizing the boat. After nearly two hours of discussion between the authorities and Glyn, the police decided we could have our passports returned in exchange for the promise never to return. We could not have been more relieved, for we had no desire ever to return.

There were nine of us finally aboard. Cheering on the dock were Vanessa and Carol Angier, a British writer who had hoped in the last moment to join us, along with Arthur, Allison, Diane, and a dozen or so AP and local reporters who wished us well and cheered. The banners were put out, the aid we were carrying displayed. After a short time, we set sail. I had gathered a duffel bag of therapeutic toys for child therapy at the Gaza Mental Health Center. Email communications between the center and myself helped clarify what was needed in order to work with the children who suffered terribly from stress disorders and mental illness after Operation Cast Lead. Two years later, I would witness personally the effects of the siege of Gaza on the population and especially the children, who make up more than fifty percent of the Gaza population. In addition, the boat carried some medicine, a few water purifiers, children's books, and some daypacks. But our true mission was our solidarity as Jews with the suffering Palestinian people in Gaza.

I was the only American. In addition to myself, the crew and passengers were:

- Glyn Secker, United Kingdom. He was the boat's captain and is a member of Jews for Justice for Palestinians.

- Reuven Moskovitz, Israel. Reuven is a a founding member of the Jewish-Arab village Neve Shalom (Oasis of Peace) and a Holocaust survivor.
- Rami Elhanan, Israel. Rami is a founding member of the The Parents Circle—Families Forum, an organization for families who lost their loved ones to the conflict. He lost his daughter Smadar to a suicide bombing in 1997.
- Dr. Edith Lutz, Germany. Edith is a peace activist and nurse, and was a passenger on the first boat to Gaza in 2008, which made a remarkably successful landing in Gaza.
- Yonatan Shapira, Israel. Yonatan is Itamar's brother and is an ex-IDF pilot and refusenik.
- Itamar Shapira, Israel. Itamar is Yonatan's brother and was a member of the boat crew.
- Eli Osherov, Israel. Eli is a reporter from Israel Channel 10 News.
- Vish Vishvanath, United Kingdom. Vish is a photographer based in London. (He has kindly given permission to use his photographs in this book; all photos appearing in this chapter were taken by him.)

The organization in Gaza ready to welcome us was the Palestinian International Campaign to End the Siege on Gaza. The director, a Gaza psychiatrist, Dr. Eyad al-Sarraj, had been a consultant to the Palestinian delegation at the 2000 Camp David Summit. He was also a recipient of the Physicians for Human Rights Award, a wonderful man of peace. I could not help but feel excited when a message came over satellite phone to let us know they awaited us and were praying for our safe arrival.

I cannot tell you what it has meant for me to be on this little catamaran, only thirty-six feet long, together in solidarity with these activists. We were one in our longing to reach Gaza. The promise of nonviolence from our passengers and crew filled me with strength and great courage. We would not incite the pirates.

Glyn Secker.

Reuven Moskovitz.

Rami Elhanan.

Dr. Edith Lutz.

Yonatan Shapira.

Itamar Shapira.

Eli Osherov.

Vish Vishvanath.

Lillian Rosengarten.

The boat itself was small and compact. There was a tiny room with a double bed where Rami and Reuven slept. In another small room, I slept on a narrow berth, while Glyn had a spot on the floor in his sleeping bag. Sleep came easily, and I was grateful for my own space. Vish secured his spot on the bench of our small galley that also functioned as a respite from the sun and a place to hang out. Next to it a step led down to a tiny, well-equipped kitchen. The others slept outside, and someone always navigated the course at the wheel. A tiny bathroom with a sink and toilet included instructions from Glyn on how to use the toilet to prevent breakdown. It would take approximately thirty-six hours to Gaza, the speed about five miles an hour. Leaving Famagusta, the Turkish flag was flying. Some hours later, we noticed the Greek police coming toward us. Because we had entered Greek waters, the Turkish flag still up was suspicious. They trailed behind us for a while and Glyn told them we were going to an Egyptian port, El Arish, as he hoisted up a Greek flag. Fortunately, they stopped pursuing us. At about 5 p.m. the sun was still strong, and the heat moved some of us into the hull, where we

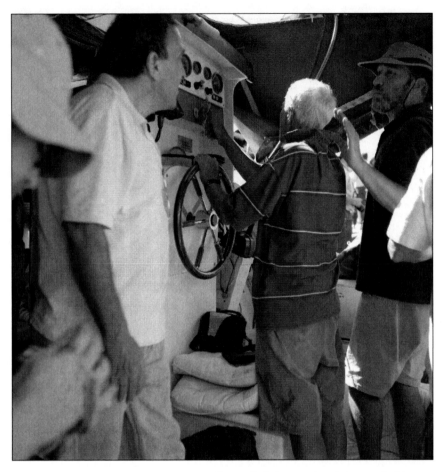

Glyn at the helm, Rami and Yonatan looking on.

relaxed, excited to be on our way. We had two satellite phones on board, and we passed one to Reuvan when CNN called. There was plenty of Israeli coverage, and Eli spoke with Channel 10. There were calls from Gaza, from the NGOs (nongovernmental organizations), a representative spoke with Yonatan and welcomed us. Not once did I doubt the sincerity of their welcoming messages. I trusted our mission as one that would create one small bond of understanding between us with the message that not all Jews support the Zionist

Lillian prepares a Palestinian flag to hoist on the boat.

agenda of occupation and destruction. We did not want to reinforce the Israeli belief that their actions represented all Jews. We were not those Jews.

Within the first few hours, Glyn taught us how to use the toilet and the water supply. He and Yonatan taught us to put on life preservers. The crew and Glyn took turns preparing meals. The first evening we had a bowl of rice and vegetables, cheese and bread, tea or coffee. We sat together in a circle watching the sea and hoping we would not be intercepted. The camaraderie was special, for we knew each one of us respected the other for our commitment to human rights and that as Jews we could not support a country we all once hoped would be a beacon of light for the world to emulate. I wrote a short poem that evening:

Chatting after dinner on the boat.

Israel!
You have risen from ashes of the Holocaust
To become your own enemy.
We weep for you, we weep for Palestine.
Israel!
You should have learned so well
Man's inhumanity to man.
Hate is hell.
Palestine!
We come to you, we are your brothers and sisters.

The next afternoon, beautiful, golden sunlight shone on the Mediterranean. Still in international waters, forty miles from Israeli waters, we jumped into the warm sea, swam, and rejoiced at this

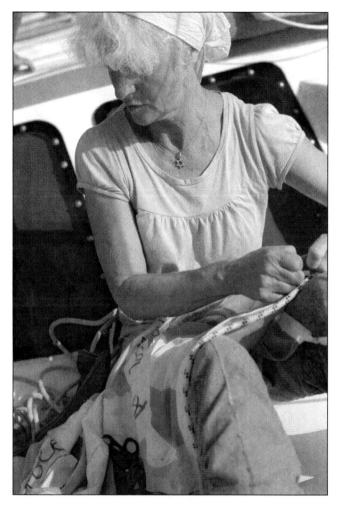

Edith prepares flags to hang on the boat.

moment of joy together in the calm waters as tiny waves rippled around us. At 6 p.m., the sun began to set, and we were now flying the Palestinian flag. At the same time, we contemplated the arrival of the IDF. Would they come during the night like the *Mavi*? Would they circle us in their helicopters and swing down onto our little boat with ropes wearing masks and carrying guns? Would they hurt us?

*Our wonderful Reuven plays his harmonica, while Rami looks on
and the moonlight reflects on the sea.*

In an amazing, surreal moment, as I watched the Palestinian flag
fly in the wind on the mast, I understood why I was here, a mission
more important than a vague fear of death. After supper, Glyn prepared us for an interception, which could happen at any moment. We
knew at the first sighting of the IDF we would put on life jackets. We
each would carry a little bag with water, medications, or anything
we might personally need. We prepared them that evening. The rest
we would leave on the boat. Our power was our group. We were not
giving up our position unless they took us by force. We would only sail
to Gaza. We would resist, but nonviolently. This is passive resistance,
the balance between resistance and nonviolence. We would not sub-
mit to them. Monday night, I slept well. The Israelis had not been
seen in international waters, and we were on track to get to Gaza in
about five hours. We would sit together arm in arm and would not be
hurt, for the whole world was watching. We grew close and dreamed
our mission would be successful. We ate and sang songs as Reuven
accompanied us on the harmonica. He played harmonica with such

The boat decorated with flags.

pathos and beauty. His playing expressed the depth of his being, his struggles and his hope. A year later, Glyn and Reuven would visit me in my log house in the Hudson Valley when they were on a speaking tour. I joined them for one wonderful evening where we three spoke in Woodstock. Edith also visited me. They are my treasured friends. On the boat we laughed, talked, and felt the excitement of our mission. We sewed flags together as Glyn, Itamar, and Yonatan hung them up on the mast. It was a most harmonious yet surreal time, sailing on the Mediterranean with a mission I felt was an expression of love for I believe in freedom, and in order to achieve freedom we must strive not to hate. Edith and I wrote in our diaries, two women brought together by fate. I now feel a special lasting bond with the passengers on the *Irene*.

On that fateful Tuesday morning, our third day, we approached Gaza waters. The weather was beautiful, ripples of gold from the rising sunlight reflected on the Mediterranean. It was the day we would have reached Gaza, and we were now close to twenty miles from shore but still in international waters. We fastened the banners Edith had sewn by hand. Glyn, Edith, and I connected them to ropes, and when we ran out, we used string. Imagine forty-two flags with eighty-four doves and more than 100 names of the people who had wanted to accompany us. How beautiful they looked and what a gift from Edith, who had sewn them by hand.

Soon, we saw guns and war paraphernalia on warships that moved toward us. It was a frightening sight. Surely, this could not really be happening? I imagined I was watching a war movie. Several smaller frigates moved too close—in the front, back, and on both sides of us. What act of insanity could this be? I imagined myself escaping, our unprotected boat of tired Jews surrounded by the Nazi navy, but I moved quickly away from this thought.

Strangely, in the background, a fleet of four or five pleasure sailboats glided along as if unconscious of the surrounding occurrence. It was ludicrous to see sailboats sharing the waters with warships, an acknowledgment of the actions of the IDF and complicit pleasure boats. We put on our life vests and sat down together with our personal belongings. Eight war ships headed toward us.

We sat together, arms linked, and sang, "We shall overcome." I was afraid. We had rehearsed our strategy of nonviolent but passive resistance. Shortly after, we received a call from the frigate asking about our intentions. Glyn informed them we were headed for Gaza port, that we were in international waters and had no intention of entering Israeli waters. They replied that Gaza was within a prohibited area and insisted we must change our course. Glyn stated we were in accordance with international law and that we were

One of the smaller Israeli military boats that approached the Jewsh Boat to Gaza.

unarmed with no materials that could be put to military use. He also told them we were carrying a consignment of aid for Gaza, and we expected safe passage. They then warned us they would intercept and this could be dangerous for the crew and damaging for the boat. Glyn reiterated that as a British flagged boat, they had no legal right to intercept and that we intended to maintain our course to Gaza. They were soon next to us, and Itamar told them in Hebrew, "We are peace activists."

The warship approached and drew parallel to the *Irene*, and a number of smaller ships were spotted coming from the east. The Navy asked us again about our intentions. We responded that we were headed for Gaza.

The Navy replied with the same declaration they made before attacking the *Mavi Marmara*: "You are entering an area which is under military blockade and is closed under international law."

Itamar replied by reading our declaration in English and Hebrew:

We are a boat of the European organization Jews for Justice for Palestinians. We are unarmed and nonviolent and determined to proceed to the port of Gaza. You are enforcing an illegal blockade, and we do not recognize your right to do this. On this Jews for Justice for Palestinians boat are peace activists of all ages, among us Holocaust survivors, bereaved parents, and Israelis who refuse to collaborate with the illegal occupation of Palestine.

The Navy repeated their message in Hebrew as their boats began to move in, eight in total. Some of the ships even had cannons.

Seeing this, we called out a message to the soldiers:

We call on you IDF soldiers and officers to disobey the illegal orders of your superior officers. For your information, the occupation of Gaza and the Palestinian Territories are illegal under international law; therefore you risk being tried in the international courts. The blockade as well as the occupation is inhumane and contradicts universal and Jewish moral values. Use your conscience. Remember our own painful history. Refuse to enforce the blockade. Refuse to occupy Palestine.

Itamar continued reading this statement on the radio as the boats came toward us. We held hands and prepared ourselves as Vish took photographs and filmed.

The boats contained in total about 100 soldiers and continued to move forward as they had threatened. Glyn remained calm and stayed the course.

The military spoke to Itamar directly and stated that he was responsible for the harm that would come to us and the risk that we were taking by not changing course. We understood we were about to be boarded at any moment. The small frigates surrounded us, and then the north side jumped on board.

All I could think was, why are these warships coming to board our little catamaran with eight Jews (and one non-Jew), mostly in their sixties, seventies and eighties? How did it come to this? What

Gyln cuts off the Jewish Boat's fuel supply.

insanity brought these soldiers—dressed to the gills with high boots, tasers, guns, helmets, and gloves—to take over our boat, in essence to kidnap us?

One soldier ripped apart our beautiful flags with quick, angry movements. He tore down the British flag too. Was any of this legal? We huddled close together in our life vests and sang "We Shall Overcome."

Although the Israeli press described the kidnapping of our boat as without incident, this was untrue despite our stance of passive resistance and nonviolence. It was impossible for me not to feel fear. I tried to find humanity in the faces of the soldiers as they boarded, in order to humanize the situation. They had apparently been waiting for us to cross the boundary of their unilaterally declared prohibited zone. It felt crazy that they were now boarding in large numbers simultaneously from both sides. At that moment, Glyn cut the engines and some of us sat over the access points to the cut-offs to prevent them restarting the engines. Then Glyn was surrounded by three commandos as he attempted to hold on to the wheel as hard as he could. One grabbed his left arm, another his right arm. A third stood by with a taser. After a struggle, the commandos managed to pull Glyn's hands from the wheel as they threw him down onto the ground and pulled away the engine key he had clutched his hand. I could not believe my eyes. It was a brutal nightmare and completely unnecessary. They, with their steely eyes, ceased to be human as they dragged Itamar to their frigate, tied his hands, and kicked him until he fell flat on his back. Yonatan attempted to quiet eighty-two-year-old Reuven, who lost it when his harmonicas fell to the ground. A pacemaker inside him, he became agitated and screamed at the soldiers, "You should be ashamed of yourselves!" Luckily we rescued the harmonicas, but at that moment, I believe it was the *Mavi* murders that prevented further violence to any one of us.

Just then, one of the "moral" ones pushed Yonatan to the ground, pulled away his life jacket. He proceeded to taser him around his heart. The sound of his cry like a wounded animal is something I will never forget. They dragged his unconscious body onto the frigate. I am sure Yonatan and Itamar were targeted beforehand for being refuseniks, the true heroes of Israel. The engines now began to fail for the fuel supply was so cleverly cut off by Glyn.

After many attempts to restart the engine, the IDF took the boat in tow. The *Irene* was designed to go through the water at a maximum speed of about eight knots. They towed us through rough waters at twelve to fourteen knots. The boat bounced about violently; it was dangerous to travel at this speed. We sustained bruises and were soaked during the exhausting passage to Ashdod. There were eight or perhaps more commandos on the boat in addition to ourselves, making it grossly overloaded. We feared the boat would break up as the whole structure groaned and made cracking sounds. It was clear the commandos intended to seriously mistreat the boat. We sat anxiously in our life vests. But the wonderful boat held out for us.

NINE

Deported

They towed us to Ashdod, an Israeli port about twenty miles south of Tel Aviv, where the Israeli soldiers offered water and sandwiches. We would have none of it and sat together without moving. It was brutally hot as we were herded from the boat into a courtyard. To get to the courtyard, we were pulled up a steep stone wall like cattle, one by one. A ladder had actually been removed (odd but true). The 100-degree sun broiled over us. As I looked around, no one familiar could be seen. I was determined not to faint, despite the brutal heat. I acutely felt the unfriendliness of the guards who milled about this God-awful place. I learned later that Glyn had returned to our sad boat, which had been searched, torn apart from top to bottom, and sniffed for drugs. Fortunately, he was able to retrieve our luggage. With good foresight, Glyn had thrown all knives and sharp instruments off the boat immediately before the IDF set foot on it.

After what seemed like more than an hour, I was taken to a makeshift, tented space to be searched and questioned. My diary was confiscated. I was subjected to an intimate body search and more questions until I found myself in a well-guarded van with tightly closed shades. It was such a relief to see Edith again in the van. Her clothes were still wet despite the heat of the afternoon. She asked for the bathroom and was escorted there. We continued to wait.

Edith was hungry and requested food. We were given a bottle of water by female guards, tight-lipped and cold in their demeanor. They brought dry sandwiches Edith was able to get down. The sight of them sickened me. We had no idea what had happened to the rest of the group. Edith and I were taken to Holon, about an hour's drive to the outskirts of Tel Aviv, as the driver and his companion played high-decibel music, loud enough to hurt our ears. We asked to have it lowered, to no avail. All we could do was acknowledge Israel as a state of collective mental illness. I perceived we were seen by our jailors as no friends to Israel, rather as anti-Semites or even possibly terrorists. It was ludicrous. Here was a reality of Jew against Jew. I thought about the *kapos*, Jewish guards in the concentration camps, Jews forced to oversee Jewish prisoners. They had tried to stay alive, to save their own skin. Threatened by Nazi guards, they sold their souls to survive. But in Israel, it is different. No guards are fighting for their lives. Indoctrinated since their school days, Israeli children are taught to hate Palestinians, or "Arabs" as they are called as terrorists and enemies of the State of Israel who threaten Israel's survival. It seems so black and white, so ignorant for children to learn to dehumanize and hate. Israeli children are brainwashed from a young age. It is muddled in my mind, the connection—*kapos* and Israeli soldiers. Is it the threat of annihilation that links both together for me?

Five elderly Jews arrested by Jews. I asked stupidly and naively, "Why?" We had longed to reach Gaza, and through our communications with Eyad al-Sarraj, as well as others from the PNGO (Palestinian non-governmental organizations), we learned that preparations were being made for our arrival. Here is beautiful fragment of a note I received from Dr. Sarraj after my deportation: "We must stay on the side of justice with tolerance, love, and peace for all."

How wonderful it would have been if we had landed to express solidarity through our mutual humanity and forgiveness. This is what we had come to offer—not as Jewish enemies to a population that has become victim to a harsh and racist Israeli system, not as Jews who claim Palestinian land as theirs through force, violence and occupation, and not as Jews who express pride at their "moral" army, an army that is designed to crush.

Nurit Peled-Elhanan is the wife of Rami Elhanan. She passed along the following report to *Mondoweiss* (10/4/2010):

Coming out of the police investigation, Yonatan [Shapira] looked like someone coming out of a prisoners' camp. Long, pale, distorted face. It was the same monstrous soldiers who attacked the *Marmara*. They were all after him. They beat him up, kicked him, and used a Taser on him. The other passengers said he was palpitating and screaming like a wounded animal, but the monster wouldn't stop. When Rami asked him for his name, he said "Gepeto." Now Rami is accused of threatening a soldier because he said he would find out his name and press charges against him. Yonatan and Itamar [Shapira, Yonatan's brother], who were handcuffed and dragged and then thrown violently to another boat, are charged with assaulting the soldiers and resisting arrest. There were dozens of fully armed commandos who attacked them on the boat, 4 navy war boats.

A very senior general, Amidror, head of research unit of the IDF said on the radio two days ago that Yonatan Shapira, an ex-pilot in the Air force is psychopath[ic] and should be locked away. I reacted to that, so they interviewed me the day after. I told them this is [what] the Russians did to Sakharov and that Yonatan is Israel's best son and an example to young people of what they should be as well, etc.

However, it seems the media are very eager to interview us, along with their complete faith in what the IDF says. We were interviewed all day long, while waiting for them to come out of the investigation, by everybody, all the time, but it looks like they see us as a curiosity rather than reliable sources of information.

The whole world should support Yonatan and Itamar Shapira now because the security forces are surely after them and there are no limits to what these soldiers would do if ordered.

Now we were treated as traitors, people to be rid of. I was arrested, fingerprinted, and photographed. I received contempt from those who guarded me. A young immigration officer questioned me as a criminal. "Are you Jewish?" he asked with an attitude of indifference and disgust. Was this the Nazi era? Would I receive a yellow star to sew on my coat?

"I am a refugee from the Nazis," I said. "I am the last generation alive to tell the story." Did he believe me? Did he listen?

He asked again, "Are you Jewish?"

I wanted to respond, but my words remained stuck in my throat: Do you need to see a number on my arm to believe me? Do you need to take blood that will register Jewish? Can you tell people's religion by their blood type or perhaps it should be stamped on my forehead? So what if I am? Was he Jewish? Did it matter what my ethnicity or religion was? What if I had been Palestinian? Would I be in a prison without any charges for the next thirty years of my life? I knew I would never feel safe again in this forlorn and dangerous land.

I am a witness to another side of Zionism that is Jew against Jew, a state gone crazy. Paranoia stokes fear so that such perpetual violence blazing from the Zionist agenda will eventually play out its own self-destruction. Most tourists who visit Israel do not see outside the myth of it as a beautiful, free democracy.

I was told by my captors I could return home if I signed a form that stated I was due to be deported for being in Israel illegally. I chose deportation, though I was very conflicted to leave Edith there. I would have been reluctantly willing to stay if Edith agreed to it, but she did not. She encouraged me to get out. I wondered why I did not question the form instead of signing so willingly. I had no access to a lawyer until later. The deportation process was humiliating. Jew against Jew, divided against one another. It pains me to describe Israel in this way. Once I had hoped for an open society where everyone who had ever been haunted or hunted could live together freely without fear.

Glyn, with courageous conviction, did not agree to sign the statement. He did not wish to recognize the Israeli law that had created a blockade as the reason for deportation. He questioned the legitimacy of the statement and could even laugh in the inspector's faces, something my temperament would not allow of me. When he was told he could add comments to the form and receive a photocopy, he added a clause stating he did not recognize the legal basis for deportation as it had no relevance in international law. I thought he was brave and smart, and that I was cowardly to have signed so quickly. I did not have the capacity to formulate such a clause and therefore capitulated. I do not feel that I was strong enough in this instance. The only other person in the signing room with me had been Edith, who also decided not to sign and be imprisoned in protest. Eventually I met with a lawyer, Smadar Ben Natan, which was arranged by JFJFP, as well as a representative from the U.S. consulate. I entered the room and burst into tears. Lydia had been contacted and told I was safe. I was reassured that they were doing all they could. I felt relief. Still concerned about Edith, I was assured that she would have a lawyer to represent her.

Immediately after, I picked up my pack, which had been stored with about thirty other bags and taken to the detention center at Ben Gurion Airport. There I met up with Glyn and Vish, who greeted me with relief. Once again, I was given an extensive body search and then began to feel angry. The luggage was inspected over and over again. What did they hope to find in my daypack? How did these small minds engage in such mindless searches day after day? It was an absurdity. I tried to find the humanity in their behavior but saw only automatons.

Accompanied by guards, I was taken to a cell, pushed in as the metal door with a small peephole slammed shut. I was thirsty and overcome with exhaustion. The dank and gray room had a locked window with bars. It smelled bad. There was a sink, toilet, dirty shower, table, chair, and bunk bed. I sat on the chair, isolated, alone, and exhausted. I used the toilet and found I was being watched. There was no privacy. I needed to lie down for just a few minutes as fatigue took over. I had pulled the semblance of a ragged blanket over me and woke up at 4 a.m., disoriented and unclear as to where I was.

I was taken from the cell by two very unfriendly guards into a van. I did not have my passport. I vaguely remember a bottle of water, and perhaps bread and cheese or some form of food, before I was taken from the cell. I don't recall having been either hungry or not. It didn't seem to matter. I was pushed into the van and headed for the plane. I turned around suddenly and noticed a frightened-looking, large, black man with his wrists chained together. I knew he was also on his way to deportation. Not a word was spoken, although I longed for contact. I turned around again and as our eyes met, I touched his hand briefly in a gesture of solidarity. When I saw the chains around his ankles, I was repelled. The van stopped adjacent to his plane, and I watched as his chains were removed. What could he have done to be treated in such a manner? I felt shame toward the inhumanity of "my" people who had no semblance to my vision of a civilized and democratic society. I was driven to an El Al plane, taken up the stairs, and greeted by a friendly stewardess as the guard handed her my passport. "Welcome aboard." She smiled and took me to a seat near the front of the plane. My passport was not returned until we were ready to exit in New York.

It is a complicated question, how a once hunted people become hunters, how victims become victimizers. Israel's hardline Zionists have lost their humanity, and Israel's poets must write of death, for love cannot live in the presence of racism and apartheid. As W.H. Auden said in his poem "September 1, 1939," "I and the public know/ What all school children learn/Those to whom evil is done/Do evil in return."

What about the right of return? Is not deportation what Jews have experienced throughout millennia of their existence? How can a so-called democracy not allow dissent? What is the fear, and where is the dream of Israel as a free society that we all long for in our hearts? Can we continue to justify the actions of the Israeli government in the name of the Holocaust, in the name of a deep, paranoid, and irrational fear of annihilation brought about by their own tragic history as former victims of a hate so deep, it led to the worst crimes against humanity against Jews by the Nazi government? Is the "moral" army responding to an unconscious fear of what they lived through? Are they plagued by the intention of the Nazis to ethnically cleanse the whole Jewish population as well as millions of others deemed "inferior" to the nationalistic standards of Nazi insanity?

It is time to step back and reflect, to let go of moral superiority, to remember we are all brothers and sisters to be treated with dignity and respect, to remember who we are.

I have such a problem with Zionism, some kind of distorted incarnation of what was once created to be a safe haven for Jews within a model of a secular nation state. (The desire to establish a nation-state has resulted in mass eviction of other nationalities and ethnic cleansing.) Hitler attempted to establish Germany as a nation-state by first exiling Jews and ultimately, by killing the majority of Jewish residents in Germany and in other countries he conquered. Attempting to enforce a nation-state where none truly exists results in high numbers of deaths for large minority populations and a lack of humanity to the extreme.

I rage against attempts to blur the distinction between Zionist nationalism and Jewish religion. Of course, some Jews are Zionists, but I am a secular, non-Zionist Jew who strongly believes in the separation of church and state for a country to be truly democratic. From my view, nationalism in any form is dangerous. It means exceptionalism, an attitude of moral superiority, a hotbed for racism that is heightened by propaganda.

Nothing about the caricature of Palestinian life is based on reality. It is a myth used as a means to put an end to the Palestinian "problem." Tragically, Israelis send their own children into the army to fight the "reviled, unknown enemy," and this is considered patriotic. We know Jews have suffered and have been victims. Is it that mentality behind the wall Israel has built? Are they still "victims" of paranoia and fear? I say no! Yet, this is the justification for abominable actions perpetrated on their Palestinian neighbors and gives power to the idea of a Jewish State that belongs only to Jews. This is a dangerous road, as we know.

Jews who love Israel must recognize that Jews can also do wrong, and they must question and speak up against human rights abuses. The Jewish community throughout the world, but especially in the United States and Europe, must distinguish between secular Jew and Zionist. One is a religion and the other a political ideology. This gives permission to dissent, to stand up and say "No," and to debate the issues from a human rights perspective. To support the apartheid directives and the brutal forms of ethnic cleansing is to do an enormous disservice to those who refuse to resist for fear of being labeled anti-Semitic. What needs clarification is that the blinded supporters of Zionist Israel are by the very nature of their support complicit with Zionist Israel's war crimes. To pretend Israel is a peace-loving democracy is to be cajoled into a deception that Israel is something it is not. Most important, claiming what has been done to the Palestinians by the Zionists is done in the name of Jews is false. What is being done to Palestinians by the Israeli Zionists will never be in my name as a Jew.

TEN

Gaza

I attempted twice to go to Gaza. The first time I had hoped to go together with Edith. It was then the Arab Spring uprising began. I felt a wild thrill to observe this momentous time. Egyptians from all walks of life responded to a movement by the younger generation to courageously stand up for reform and demand the departure of Mubarak and his henchmen. The capacity for mass communication via Twitter and other cyber means demonstrated the power of the internet to organize protest movements. Censorship and deceit after decades of dictatorship could no longer be tolerated. So phenomenal was this uprising, I fervently hoped it would change the course of Egypt and move it toward a more open and equitable society. Of course, I dreamed that a successful revolution would support a strong movement to free Gaza. The United States has long supported right-wing governments and is not known to have stood behind social revolutions. Corrupt dictators cloak abuses under the thinly veiled guise of "democracy." The word has lost all meaning and has become a metaphor for occupation, corruption, and the undermining of social change. Who could have known during the fervor of the popular uprising in Tahrir Square that it would fail and the democratically elected president, Mohammed Morsi, would be overthrown (and sentenced to death) by Mubarak's former army? General Sisi, a close confidant of Mubarak, was not elected but seized power. I am deeply troubled by Morsi's overthrow, with U.S. approval. With Morsi as president, Palestinians in Gaza had an ally. I believe under Morsi, Egypt could have had a major influence on supporting Palestinians against their occupiers. In contrast, Sisi has withdrawn his support and is a friend of Israel. Sisi's government is replete with violence and human rights abuses. I identify with the feeling of being caged, a loss of freedom. My empathy is with the struggle to become free of a government's violent human rights abuses. Gaza Palestinians, a caged population, needed Egyptians to be their ally. This is now lost to more corruption. I accepted the need to cancel this first attempt to see Gaza with hesitation. The gates of Rafah, the border crossing between Egypt and Gaza, were closed at the time, and Edith and I would not have been allowed in. I was however hopeful that Egypt, in the throws of a revolution against Mubarak, could, with an elected leader, stand with the Palestinian struggle without allegiance to the United States and Israel. This dream ended swiftly.

I am thinking about one Saturday evening in April 1999. Phil had been dead for three years and I spent an afternoon walking around in his old neighborhood. I have always loved the Village, and for a time I lived on Washington Square with Frank and our three children. After Phil died, I moved from the Village to the Upper West Side. It became increasingly difficult to pass Phil's old apartment at 145 Sullivan Street, where once we had felt so much hope. Since 2001, I have left the city, and I now live in my log house in the woods in upstate New York. I have lost my desire to return to 145 Sullivan Street. It is when Phil enters my conscious awareness that I feel once again the ice in my veins and grief that can never dissipate completely. Yet in some inexplicable way, I am less alone as I identify with all parents of the world who have lost children, but especially under the brutal Israeli occupation. This is when I wonder how it is that Jews who have been so victimized feel the right to occupy and disenfranchise another people.

How I lift myself out of the morass is to use the memory of Phil to pull me along in my often desperate search to understand why life ceases to be precious if you are a Palestinian in occupied Palestine or black in South Africa or Jewish along with other undesirables in Nazi Germany. Phil's gift to me is my insistence to search for truth and not to hide from fear that is capable of distorting reality.

Because the *Irene* was abducted by the Israeli Defense Forces in September 2010, and because it was towed to Israeli immigration detention, our goal to reach Gaza was subverted. I planned again to travel to Gaza on February 21, 2011, intent on spreading awareness and generating support from the outside world. I needed to document in my memory the agony of people who live under siege and who had endured two weeks of incessant bombing attacks during Operation Cast Lead in 2008–2009. I needed to search for survivors, for hope amidst layers of destruction from bombs, missiles, and chemical weapons. The horror could be seen in the eyes of the children: some withdrawn, some mute, and others with stories of terror, nightmares, death, and violence. I needed to witness the destruction of infrastructure, water systems, hospitals, and schools, and understand more personally where hope came from. Because of the uprising, the Rafah border was closed, and it was reopened only at sporadic intervals. As we were not sure we would be allowed in, we postponed our trip.

Opportunity knocked once again in October 2011. A friend invited me to join a German delegation to Gaza in 2012, organized by Pax Christi. We were ten people, all German, and I was once again the only American. One member of the group was Wiltrud Rosch-Metzler, vice president of Pax Christi (Germany), an international, non-profit, nongovernmental Catholic peace movement with interests in the Middle East. She wrote in the *Jerusalem Post* in 2012: "I am not buying goods with the origin specification 'Israel' because under this designation products could come from the settlements." Wiltrud's message was especially important, for criticism of the Israeli political agenda is not well-tolerated in Germany

Our group included three men who had been passengers on the *Mavi Marmara*. I found it amazing that four out of a group of ten passengers had been on sailing vessels intending to break the siege of Gaza. They were: Matthius Jocheim, psychiatrist and activist, from Frankfurt; Norman Paech, retired law professor, progressive activist and member of the Bundestag until 2009, from Hamburg; and Nader al-Sakka, born in Gaza and president of the Palestinian Community in Hamburg where he lived now. Nader's return to Gaza was his first since he left as a child, and it was a deeply emotional experience. His family in Gaza had been prosperous landowners and businessmen. We visited an arid area his family had once owned—acres of land for farming. Now barren and lifeless, small remnants of what may have been a wall with an arched door were all that stood of a family mosque, once a joyful place of gatherings and of prayers. The stones were reminders of a brutal history, now loosely piled and forlorn in the scorched heat of midday. Nader had returned home and wept for his lost past. Many of his family still live in Gaza today, and we met them in their gated house, ate lunch on the porch, and observed Nader's reunion with his mother, sisters, and brothers. Another brother and his family, now living in Canada, had also come to Gaza for this special occasion. Now Nader, in 2015, has been refused entrance into Gaza since our 2012 journey. I am told this weighs very heavily on him. Now he remains in Hamburg, banned from returning to Gaza.

We all initially met in a modest hotel in Cairo. The pyramids and sphinx I had put on my agenda of notable sites to visit bore no similarity to any fantasies I may have harbored. Rather, I found a tourist trap. In order to reach the pyramids themselves, we were required to hire a camel or horse as well as a guide and a young boy to lead the camel. To walk there, although not far, would have been too hot and difficult through the rough, sandy terrain. Riding the camel was not particularly pleasant when one of my sandals slipped off and the camel decided to sit down. It took some effort to move the animal as I sweltered on this strange, smelly beast of burden. The final cost amounted to $80 for each of us. I justified this with the awareness that people needed to earn a living. There is a reason for telling the pyramid story: I had arranged an appointment to obtain an affidavit at the Consulate in Cairo from the American Citizen's Service so as to expedite my entrance into Gaza. I will never understand why I chose not to go. Did I think it would not be needed? I had an appointment set up, and I miscalculated my actions. I would pay for my neglect later at the Rafah gate.

While still in Cairo, I visited Tahrir Square and walked along the Nile and Embassy Row. There had been extensive damage to the Israeli Embassy, which was now evacuated. Thousands had marched recently from Tahrir Square during a protest to express frustration about the lack of changes and continued government violence by Egypt's ruling generals. Several protesters had broken through a wall built to protect the embassy, and they succeeded in entering the building. They threw files from the windows, burned an Israeli flag, and replaced it with Egyptian and Palestinian flags.

Nader arranged for a car rental for the six-hour drive from Cairo to Rafah. The gates would be open only until noon. At 5:45 p.m., we were still at the crossing at the gate, thoroughly exhausted. The others had acquired permission to enter. Their documents, expedited together, had everything in order. It was I who could not get through, and I was frantic. I needed the missing affidavit and tried with desperation to call the embassy from my phone, which failed to work. The others, although sympathetic, were ready to go without me. I pleaded with the guard who spoke no English. At my wit's end, I had the wherewithal to ask Nader to translate something I wanted to say to the Egyptian officer in charge. I spoke with much emotion and tears running down my face. I said, "I was on the Jewish Boat and could not get into Gaza. I am Jewish and wanted to express my solidarity with the Palestinian struggle for freedom. I was arrested by the Israeli Navy, towed to Israel, and thrown out, deported. Now I cannot get into Gaza because of some piece of paper. I do not belong anywhere, neither with Israelis or Palestinians." To my enormous relief, I was given permission to enter. I took great care of the large duffel bag I would donate to the Gaza Mental Health Center, therapeutic toys to be used when working with traumatized children.

Soon I witnessed with my own eyes this sad place called Gaza, where the majority of its population live in a squalid hell. What haunts me today in addition to the trauma of Cast Lead is the fifty days of ceaseless bombing, deaths, and destruction in 2014 named ludicrously "Operation Protective Edge." What is left of Gaza now? Infrastructure in rubbles, over 2000 dead, and a completely traumatized population. I could not have imagined at the time of my visit that Israel, the land of terror, would nearly obliterate the caged population and with such brutal force.

In the refugee camps, children were everywhere and played in the rubble of the ashen earth. Their beautiful faces haunt me. The local population that spoke English embraced me as a Jew, and our humanity resonated for we as Semites know suffering. It was important to identify myself as Jewish in order to validate to the caged ones that not all Jews are occupiers and that we do not all hate Palestinians. Particularly interesting to me was my strong identification with the population of the open-air prison. The Gaza ghetto where one exists locked out of life was our mutual experience as was my identification with the Palestinian refugee trauma.

With the children, we spoke with our eyes. They were ragged and charming like children everywhere but like few children anywhere. I wonder often what will become of these children after so much brutalization. How will they help to heal the world, and can they grow up not to hate? A note of optimism I must include here: I have just read a book that leaves me marveling at creativity that continues to live in tandem with suffering. It is the creativity of the young writers who told their sad and poignant stories in *Gaza Writes Back: Short Stories from Young Writers in Gaza, Palestine* (Just World Books, 2014) that gives me hope.

There was an evident class system in Gaza. I attended a beautiful engagement party one evening at our hotel. The women were beautifully dressed, and the men of the family were prosperous, conducting successful businesses. I was invited to join them, and it was an extravaganza. The women wore beautiful long dresses, their hair done up elegantly: a band played for dancing, and yes, it was beautiful. I thought how implausible, this wealth exists side by side with the horrors of the occupation. Why was I so surprised? There is a ruling class in every form of society no matter how battered.

There was a common theme of physical abuse within families. Harsh, squalid conditions, lack of work opportunities, and use of drugs (there is an underground market) all create anger and hopelessness. Ghetto families are caught within generations of racist disregard for human life and an extraordinarily brutal form of collective punishment. There is also another side of the Palestinian struggle in Gaza: dedicated men and women who work side by side in medicine, social work, education, law, and construction. Following too many generations of trauma, their pride and hopes for freedom are something to see. These live alongside hopelessness, death, and destruction. I met many Palestinian professionals, men and women working together, as lawyers, human rights activists, and politicians from both the Fatah and Hamas parties, engineers, professors. I saw schools completely destroyed after Cast Lead, rebuilt again, as well as hospitals. Here is where the importance of the tunnels emerges: there could have been no building material without the tunnels, for equipment could not freely get into Gaza. I saw littered streets with garbage flowing and was witness to areas where children had been blown up by missiles as they ran to escape the bombings of their schools. It is difficult to believe if one has not seen it, so brutal is life in Gaza. Life now is surely more brutal after the 2014 barrage of bombs and chemicals said to have been used on the population as experiments supported by the United States—truly devastating as I struggle against hopelessness that for me can only be countered with actions against the occupation.

Palestinians in Gaza are a dignified people and to witness their suffering as well as the work they do for their community is beyond anything I have ever known. It remains a moral question how decades of brutalization and punishment can be met with silence, and complicity in the West including even the churches.

What is destroyed with each new generation is the hope that children can live without war and hate.

Gaza life exists in a cage kept mostly isolated from the world. Its citrus trees have been uprooted. Flowers are no longer exported, nor are vegetables, fruits, or olives, formerly a thriving export business. Since 2000, the Israeli army has destroyed 114,000 olive trees. Many of the rest were destroyed during Cast Lead. (One can barely fathom the destruction to infrastructure, the massive death toll, and destruction of houses and services in the Gaza ghetto during the fifty days of bombings in 2014.)

Farming is difficult and in some areas impossible. Much of Gaza looked like a war zone when I was there, bullet holes visible on the sides of buildings. The area lacked proper sewage pumps. Mediterranean waters are infested with raw sewage, while a three-mile limit, closely watched by the Israeli navy (and presently also by the Egyptian navy), has collectively destroyed a once flourishing fishing industry. After the sewage systems were destroyed, a project to upgrade coastal sewage plants was initiated in 2010. It was then halted because Israel would not send concrete. Through NGOs, the UN, World Bank, France, Italy, and Germany contributed to rebuild the sewage systems. The difficulty is that donors must not only contribute money but also implement the projects. Any building that took place along the three-mile green line (boundaries between Israel, West Bank, and Gaza), where sludge work is in progress, requires daily Israeli permission. The bombings in 2014 left indescribable horror to the Gazan population. The EU, in particular Germany, along with the United States continues to send arms of destruction. It is big business. We weep and the world looks on.

It is the grimmest of war stories, telling of unimaginable horror where tunnels and miles of mazes once functioned to alleviate suffering and sustain life. Goods were brought in from Egypt through dangerous tunnels, regularly bombed by rockets or blown up. The men who worked in the tunnels took daily chances on their lives. Diesel oil and gasoline were pumped through the tunnels at a third of the prices the Israelis charge. In addition, building materials, cement, medicines, bandages, first aid, even cars and washing machines found their way into Gaza. Articles sent through Ashdod, Israel, often must wait months before they are inspected and may never arrive in Gaza. The tunnels have been destroyed. (By 2013, many of the tunnels had been destroyed by the Egyptian government; as if 2015, all have been destroyed.) Without tunnels, there is total paralysis in rebuilding construction and goods, which further isolates Gaza into a hell without resources.

Electricity remained scarce when I was there, and backed-up generators used in hospitals could turn on twelve times a day. In

2015, electricity and water are far scarcer. Generators consistently break down during surgery. Repair of generators and equipment in general is a difficult problem because replacements take months to arrive from donating countries. The same is true of new imaging equipment that stands idle when even the smallest repair is needed. Once something breaks down, there is a wait, usually of more than a year, for replacements, which come from participating NGO countries that support Palestine.

Those who are ill are unable to receive advanced treatments. Forty percent of medications for necessary treatment were not available in 2012. Now the situation is more dire, a tragedy that has befallen a profoundly oppressed people. In Hebron I am told there is a sign: "There is no Palestine and there never will be." Do Jews who have been victimized have the right morally to occupy and disenfranchise another people?

Chemotherapy drugs, too expensive, do not exist in Gaza. Also missing are gloves, needles, sutures, antibiotics, and the most basic necessities. Some wheelchairs are donated from participating countries. They are in working condition for the many young people who have had limbs blown off. I was told at the Jabaliya clinic that several shipments of wheelchairs sent by Israel had parts missing. On and on it goes, the human misery. Yet the work going on there is nothing less than extraordinary. I met a young woman whose leg had been blown off. She was studying communications to be a journalist and to expose the plight of her people to the world. There is a sizable populations of college graduates. I met remarkable women doing service work, setting up local clinics, working with prison families.

Only the sickest, most vulnerable patients in need of advanced treatments are sent to Israeli hospitals. The trip is long and arduous with many checkpoints, so many cannot survive. Patients who have cancer cannot receive chemotherapy; medicines are scarce. I saw a woman who had had a bilateral mastectomy for breast cancer who, unless she was able to be transferred to an Israeli or Egyptian hospital, could not receive chemo drugs. Now it has become almost impossible to get out of Gaza for treatment. Children, unaccompanied by parents, can easily die before transfer. Most cruel is when parents are not given permission to accompany them. Patients in the past were more readily sent via Rafah to Cairo for treatment, but this has become increasingly difficult in the post-Morsi political climate. Tragically, travel to hospitals both in Egypt and Israel remains even more elusive, difficult, lengthy, and fraught with danger.

Al-Shifa Hospital (meaning "healing" in Arabic) is the largest and main referral hospital in the Gaza Strip. It had 700 beds in 2012 and saw 1,200 patients a day. The effect of the Israeli siege on health has been nothing less than devastating. I was exceedingly impressed with the commitment of the hospital staff. Following Operation Cast Lead, Shifa Hospital was completely destroyed and then rebuilt more than once. Depleted uranium and white phosphorus were found after three weeks of endless bombings night and day. I met teachers in the Save Our Children project who worked with two eight-year-old boys who were left unable to speak two years after Operation Cast Lead. One still finds chemicals in the soil and in the bodies of the children who are born prematurely with cancer and disfigurement. After Cast Lead, samples from the soil, the water, and the bodies of children were tested. Thirty-three toxic materials were found in the ground that are linked to sterility, cancer, disfigurement of embryos, and miscarriages. I saw maimed children in the Palestine Medical Relief Society clinic in the Jabaliya refugee camp. Deformed and often disabled children had their childhoods and lives stolen from them as parents sadly tended them and waited for a miracle. Too many babies were miscarried or born with body parts missing. I tell you, one must see it to believe the harm carried out in the name of a safe, Jewish-only state. I shudder to think of what the continuous brutalization of this young generation in Gaza will lead to in the coming years.

We met with Joe Catron, a young American who has worked with the fishermen. He showed us the *Oliver*, a boat that accompanies fisherman, who are continuously fired upon by the Israeli navy. The fishermen are harassed or killed, their small, meager boats seized or fired upon with water guns. This disaster for the fishermen's livelihoods continues and has worsened. Now Mediterranean waters are over-fished and polluted, and fisherman forced within a three-mile limit, although attacks still occur within the three miles (this according to the mood of the ever-menacing Israeli patrol). The *Oliver* is not fired upon for it frequently has international observers as witnesses. The *Oliver* is forbidden to help a fisherman when his boat is attacked and fired on. Joe pointed out to us the boats that had been seized, muti-lated, and then sent back to the Gaza shore completely broken. How is one to understand man's inhumanity to man in this endless cycle of occupation and hate, and what is the way to peace? It is time to end the occupation, which can only occur through pressure from the European Union, United States, and churches, who must say "No" to occupation.

There is a large and formidable university in Gaza called the Islamic University of Gaza. However, because development is not possible, 15,000 to 17,000 university graduates have few or no oppor-tunities to work.

There are unprecedented numbers of Palestinian men, women, and children who are held in Israeli prisons, many for years with no charge. I witnessed mothers, fathers, and siblings stand in weekly vigils with photographs of their imprisoned family members. Some have been gone for thirty years. We met one evening with ex-pris-oners who have formed an NGO calling for protection of Palestinian prisoners. Israel holds some 4,800 prisoners accused of inciting harm to Israel. In recent months, long-term (eight-month) hunger strikes have brought awareness and many protests in support of prison-ers. Palestinians see the prisoners as heroes in their struggle for statehood. Israelis view them as terrorists. Our group met with Abu Nasser, director of the Prisoners Ministry. He told us that since the year 2000, 9,000 children have been imprisoned, and parents are re-fused visitation rights if their children are older than sixteen. Some of the arrests have been for throwing stones or taking part in a sin-gle demonstration. Nine hundred mothers have also been arrested; 1,500 prisoners have been severely ill. And new sicknesses occur with each passing year. Children under sixteen are allowed some contact with their families. My question is, why were children arrested? And why doesn't the world speak out? We can remain silent no longer.

I met representatives from both Fatah and Hamas, and we had discussions about human rights for Palestinians. The Fatah representative I met was Dr. Abdallah Frangi, a former German minister for Fatah. He lives in Germany and in Gaza, where we were invited to lunch at his elegant apartment. Once again the contrast of wealth against despair and extreme poverty was all too evident. We met Dr. Ghazi Hamad, the Hamas deputy foreign minister at our hotel. I was interested to hear what he had to say and sat directly in front of him. As I looked into his eyes, I could see his humanity, not a terrorist but an ordinary man speaking to us about the enormous crisis in Gaza. We were having a dialogue, the only way to understand one another and resolve differences. What he said in 2012 is still salient today. The situation remains frozen; there are more settlements and more confiscation of land. He felt it was most important for Fatah and Hamas to reconcile and form a unified government. This remains difficult as it is not in the interest of Israel to create a unified force. "The split, is painful, Israel as well as radical jihadist groups take steps to prevent unification," he said. "The unanimous feeling amongst Palestinians is that no achievement is possible without unity." In 2014, unification briefly occurred, and it is believed this was a major impetus for the war crimes in Gaza. Every effort has consistently been made to prevent a unified Palestinian force that could resist the Zionist stronghold. The struggle in Gaza takes place in near complete isolation from the international community. Dr. Hamad presented a powerful image of Hamas working for the liberation of Palestine and striving for dignity and independence. He reiterated a recognition of Israel, but as an occupying power. Israel has never acknowledged themselves as occupiers. "The road to freedom," Hamad added, "requires a recognition by Israel of the 1967 borders and the right of return for Palestinian refugees." In addition, he stated that Israel has never recognized even the minimum requests of Palestinians. These issues remain stalemated, but this must change to prevent a common catastrophe. Although this is sure to be controversial, I do not see Hamas as any worse than most governments. I am not including here the violent, terrorist offshoots such as Salafis or Wahhabis, extreme and ultra-conservative militant Islamists. (It is believed that a Salafi extremist murdered Juliano Mer-Khamis, founder of Freedom Theatre in Jenin, Palestine.) Hamas is the Palestinian-elected representative of Palestinians in the occupied territories. We must extend our hand to the enemy for we are also the enemy. There is no "them" and "us."

I am deeply impressed by the beauty of the Palestinians and their drive toward dignity and freedom. So much of what I saw and heard in Gaza has left a deep, black hole in my consciousness, for I am aware that the crimes committed by Israel, and with the United States' complicity, are some of the worst crimes committed against people not seen as human beings. Instead, Palestinians are demonized and dehumanized in an attempt to obliterate their history, their dignity, and their right to exist in safety and peace. Forty-eight years of occupation must end, and voices from Germany, the United States, and churches must refuse to remain silent and must support Palestinian justice.

APPENDIX
Selected Writings

On "Anti-Semitism," War Crimes and Old Poets

Silence in the face of apartheid is unbearable.

We can no longer remain silent nor turn our backs and pretend ignorance to a gruesome occupation of stolen land where Palestinians once lived in peace.

The situation has deteriorated as we observe Jewish settlers who spew their hate with such revulsion and racism on Palestinian families, it makes my stomach turn. The United States and Europe (by example I insist) remain silent thus complicit, not daring to criticize the holier-than-thou state of Israel for fear of being called anti-Semites.

True anti-Semites rage on but they are not the human rights activists who have the courage to oppose apartheid and brutality, dissenters who challenge the cruel illegal occupation, who speak out against the outrageous destruction of a people unwanted and dehumanized for the sake of the "Democratic Jewish State," all lies in the face of a deep pathology, a state that demonizes resistance to what is meant to remain hidden. No longer is this possible, for the fate of Israel as a viable democracy rests in the acknowledgement that occupation and fear mongering lead only to death and destruction.

Indeed, the activists are heroes who have no attachment to anti-Semitism nor the vile accusation of wishing for the destruction of Israel. This is sheer paranoia and manipulation. It is urgent to examine in depth to what length Israeli Prime Minister Benjamin Netanyahu's government will continue to escalate in order to fulfill the fantasy of a Jewish State. There is no possibility to achieving this out of the ashes of Palestinians held hostage and subjected to the most brutal uprooting and forced ghetto-ization under an amoral Israeli army that has been taught to hate.

Consider how the mere suggestion of a potential Islamic State for Egypt (where church and state are also fused) sends shudders through Americans and Europeans who are taught to fear Islam as a new form of Naziism. In a closed society information is skewed and dissent is stifled. We become witness to manipulations of the general population based on lies and fear. Is this not a virulent form of domestic terrorism that that uses Islamophobia as a tool to scare people into silence, to trample debate, to destroy freedom of speech, to loathe dissent, and to label any critic of Israel's crimes as "unpatriotic" or worse yet an "anti-Semite" who wishes only for the destruction of Israel. Israel's crimes of apartheid have created a cancer, an obsession built on lies.

I cannot imagine how one justifies the human rights atrocities (carefully kept out of the U.S. news reporting and always skewed in favor of the Israelis without mentioning the occupation) committed in the name of creating a Jewish state. For those who continue to deny the horrors perpetrated, who have refused to see, who have turned their backs, it is time to drop the masks, the psychopathic pretense that Israel is only "defending " itself against destruction. From what I observe and have witnessed personally both in an Israeli prison, through my deportation, and from my trip to Gaza it is the government of Israel, the occupation, violence, ethnic cleansing, and brutalization of the Palestinian people that puts Israel at risk for continuous slaughter. Israel must face the reality that the land belongs just as rightfully to Palestinians. For this possibility to realize itself there needs to be a separation of church and state where reason can overcome the insane claim that there are no Palestinians nor Palestinian land that will be returned.

How can it continue, denial by American Jews who blindly support Israel as victims that must defend themselves? How can Zionism in its present form also be a liberal democracy?

Zionism has taken the form of a powerful nationalistic, ideologically based way of life. Its pathology is evident in the occupation and all the despair it brings to Palestinians who yearn for dignity and freedom. It is also evident in intolerance of dissent and dialogue aimed to expose the intractable hard line of the Netanyahu government.

Anti-Semitism has been distorted and relegated to the dissenters as a means to cover up the lies and crimes. I cringe to observe young Israeli soldiers and the powerful IDF as they attack Palestinian women, children, grandparents, activists calling for freedom, as if they had no beating hearts but were vermin to be stepped on. Yes! It is gruesome to observe this vile form of racism and it must be easier for some to forgive the Israelis and condemn the Palestinians.

I cannot end without mention of Günter Grass pleading for nuclear sanity and the acknowledgment of Israel as a nuclear power. This poet seeks to break the complicit silence, to break through the lies. Can he never be forgiven for his mistake when in his youth he was briefly drawn into the nationalistic fervor in another time? Can he never redeem himself for he has given the world such powerful antiwar writings including the great "Tin Drum"? We must look at how we condemn. It is easier to condemn an old poet than an occupation that exists under the nose of its deniers.

This essay first appeared on the *Palestine Chronicle* website
on October 10, 2012

Palestinian and Jew: One Humanity

For a moment, when I knew there were two ships with twenty-seven activists nearing the waters that would bring them to the shores of Gaza, I imagined no war ships would come to drag them to Ashdod, to abort the messages of solidarity and hope for Palestinians who suffer profoundly the indignities of living in the cage of Gaza. I can only speak of Gaza because I no longer visit Nablus or Ramallah or Jenin, places I had traveled to before I was banned from Israel, as another human being who happens to be a Jew who condemns the dehumanization of an entire population of Palestinians. How long must we wait before the United States decides to liberate the Palestinians and condemn Israel for its totalitarian practices under the guise of "security"?

I am afraid of the military capacity and actions by the US and its UN surrogates as well as the military capacities of Israel and the US to make wars. Palestinians have not done to Israelis what has been done to them, they have never demolished houses nor created a ghetto for Israelis. I am not afraid of Palestinians. Many do not understand me and insist that Palestinians and indeed all Muslims must be feared and reviled. I am taken aback at the denial of history and the enormous resistance to having an open dialogue on the subject. It is not difficult to observe how Israel, in order to direct attention away from the plight of the Palestinians would prefer to demonize and attack Iran, an action supported by American Jews who have been manipulated to believe that Iran must be smashed before they smash Israel. From an Israeli perspective, Iran can easily be demonized in the form of "Iran's wish to destroy Israel." The enemy (Muslims) are not granted peoplehood so as to instill fear into the hearts of many in Israel, in the American-Jewish community, and throughout many parts of Europe.

To create "fear" is a potent form of terrorism which renders people powerless. Fear obscures reality and blinds reason and empathy. If we are blind to our common humanity, the "other" is reduced to non-personhood, monster, terrorist, or without a heart. This is a form of racism whereby propaganda and terrorism become active components to maintain the status quo. It also provides a "legitimate" reason to deprive Palestinians of all legal status, a home, and a state. What the rest of the world sees is a most radical breakdown of morality and justice in a society that claims to be a democracy.

Hannah Arendt wrote during my early youth. I deeply admire her as a political thinker and a writer who forces us to think albeit not necessarily to agree. She too was a refugee from Nazi Germany and she was at ease with her identification as a Jew in the diaspora. She respected the idealism of the early Zionist organizations in Germany. In Paris Arendt worked for Youth Aliyah, a Zionist organization that rescued Jewish young people from Europe, preparing them to emigrate as agricultural workers to Palestine. As early as the 1940s, however, Arendt advocated for a binational state that would encompass Jews and Arabs as equal citizens. How many of us are aware of of how Martin Buber, Gershom Scholen, Hannah Arendt, and other German intellectuals bitterly fought against the founding of Israel as a "Jewish State." They predicted through their humanism and liberalism a new form of racism and war that would create enormous strife and tension between Israel, its protectors, and those who fought for the equality and dignity for all peoples. In those early days, Hebrew University became a base for disposing of David Ben Gurion as well as a means to discredit the conception of Israel as a Jewish State.

Throughout her career, Arendt argued for the importance of deep thinking, dialogue, and the democratic state's requirement for free discourse. Politics to her was "the gathering of citizens for expressions of genuine freedom and action." (Jessica Kraft, "Hannah Arendt.")

Tragically, dissent created fear in Israel, evident as we observe and live through the intolerance and muzzling of those dissenters who refuse to accept the paradigm created within the Zionist state concerning Israel's path to security and its behavior toward its Palestinian neighbors. Zero tolerance for dissent and dialogue creates deeper intolerance and racial inequality. As Israel continues to believe in the morality of its society and its actions, we who dissent must push deeper to understand the political and moral causes of Israel's path of dehumanization with its ongoing agenda to discredit the humanity of Palestinians, Arabs, and Muslims through racist hate and fear.

As we witness Israel's disturbing and hard-held belief that security brings peace, it seems that nothing is further from the truth for it is only peace and tolerance that bring security!

Readers, stand with me to rage against the crimes committed year after year against Palestinians who continue their brave struggle for a homeland and dignity. Not in my name shall the open-air, obscene prisons and the continuous debasement of human rights be allowed to exist.

This essay first appeared on the *Palestine Chronicle* website
on November 7, 2011

No Freedom in the Land of False Prophets

I ask, how can the Jewish State find freedom as occupier?
Two occupations have eaten Israel where mosques burn and a faux Museum
Sits on desecrated Muslim tombs. They call it Museum of Tolerance, I call it
Muslim cleansing, killer of those deemed inferior.
False prophets, destroyer of 800,000 olive and citrus plants, subjugation.
Collective abuse, fishermen attacked likes vermin by Israeli killer boats.
Apartheid! Word we dare not whisper, write or speak.
Condemned by true believers, the Zionist story makes one shudder.
I've heard the racist words before, when Jews were driven from their homes and vilified.
Now I hear it all again from a big Rabbi contender for The Jewish Heroes competition.
Asked how Jews should treat their neighbors he said:
"The only way to fight a moral war is the Jewish way. Destroy the holy sites,
Kill men, women children and cattle."
I remember another time, "No Jews Allowed." Germany nearly succeeded.
Now false prophets decree Arabs not allowed, a Zionist story.
No Palestinians to live life with dignity for "We" are the chosen people.
It's written in the Old Testament.

This poem first appeared on the *Mondoweiss* website
on Decmber 1, 2011.

Rains White Phosphorous Here

Travel with me to the land of sad oranges.
Here children play in refugee camps. Grey, grey the buildings along
the narrowest streets.
Stench of garbage, cesspools of sewage no sun, no trees.
Rains white phosphorous here where missiles fall.
White rain burns the skin and organs die.
I am haunted by their faces, eyes speak the unspeakable.
I have seen it all before.
I want to tell them soon it will be over
This tragedy for which there is no forgiveness.
They wonder who I am and so
I show a peace sign, as if to say I am a friend.
"Viva Palestina" they echo after me.

Imagine what it is like for me
Refugee from Nazi madness,
To see AGAIN proud people
Demonized as evil, driven from their land, ripped from their roots.
Grimmest of war stories.
Unimaginable horror, collective punishment, life unsustainable
As if we did not know already, how nationalism in its cruelest form
Is born of twisted hate and ideology
To cloud all forms of reason.
Sometimes I feel I have lost all reason,
That I simply dream this nightmare of Israel, echo of "death to all
Jews."
Now, "Palestinians don't exist."

This poem first appeared on the *Mondoweiss* website
on January 28, 2012.

Acknowledgments

To my children Daniel and Lydia, who witnessed many years of my struggles, rewrites, isolation, and the many incarnations until the focus and purpose for writing my story became clear. Thank you for your encouragement and patience. To my dear friends, Connie Hogarth, Ramzy Baroud, Phil Weiss, Edith Lutz, and at least another dozen who read bits and pieces of this ever-evolving story while giving me courage and support. I was again encouraged after my computer and backup were stolen in Bali. I had hoped to complete a draft but instead began from the beginning once again. Thank you.

To my first editor, Sejal Chad, who took time to read through and edit a draft despite her own time pressures. It was she who helped me to think more clearly about focus. I am grateful.

To my publisher, Helena Cobban, who believed in me, and to my editor, Diana Ghazzawi, for her wise suggestions and steady support. I can't thank you enough.

To our photographer on the Jewish Boat, Vish Vishvanath, for his friendly consent to use his photographs, those he managed to hold on to despite the attempted confiscation of all photographic material after we were towed to Ashdod by the Israeli Navy.

Thank you and with love,
Lillian

About the Author

Lillian Rosengarten is a clinical social worker and psychoanalyst. She is also a poet, writer, mother, grandmother, and progressive human rights activist. Her writings have been published on *Mondoweiss* and elsewhere. Lillian practices meditation and has traveled broadly, pursuing her interest in Buddhism and other ways of understanding the world.

Lillian with her granddaughters,
Emilia and Melina.

CPSIA information can be obtained at www.ICGtesting.com
Printed in the USA
BVOW02s0244220915

419051BV00005B/26/P